Made to Move

KNOWING AND LOVING GOD THROUGH OUR BODIES

WENDY LEBOLT

UPPER
ROOM BOOKS®
NASHVILLE

Other seeds fell on good soil and brought forth grain, some a hundredfold, some sixty, some thirty.

—Matthew 13:8

Do you not know that in a race the runners all compete, but only one receives the prize? Run in such a way that you may win it.

—1 Corinthians 9:24

In memory of Mary Anne Noland: friend, confidante, truth-speaker, action figure, and ever-faithful follower of Jesus Christ. She was the soil that grounded me and the breeze that propelled me toward the finish line of this work. On Pentecost Sunday, 2016, a mighty wind lifted her across the finish line of this life into the eternal love of God. What a race run. What an example set. What a finish. Ever, my thanks.

Contents

Introduction

One of the scribes came near and heard them disputing with one another, and seeing that [Jesus] answered [the Sadducees] well, he asked [Jesus], "Which commandment is the first of all?" Jesus answered, "The first is, 'Hear, O Israel: the Lord our God, the Lord is one; you shall love the Lord your God with all your heart, and with all your soul, and with all your mind, and with all your strength.' The second is this, 'You shall love your neighbor as yourself.' There is no other commandment greater than these."

—Mark 12:28-31

When Jesus answered the scribe's question, he affirmed that the greatest purpose of our lives is to know and love God completely. But how can we know a God we don't see? How do we love a God we can't touch? If we are meant to know and love this God, then we need an accessible, tangible, real-life way to accomplish it. God activates this in our lives by giving us bodies that are made to move.

When God created us and knit us together, though fearfully and wonderfully made (see Psalm 139), we were yet incomplete. God, throughout our lives, recreates us in our living—in the movement of our bodies, the agility of our minds, the agency of our activities, and in the subtle shifts in position or perspective that God initiates. As God moves, God inclines us to move. We may take heart in the fact that all of what we do—which radiates from God's calling on our lives—may be done solely for the purpose of knowing and loving God more. Getting to know God is more than a mental or spiritual endeavor; it's a physical one too.

Yes, we have perishable bodies that scripture tells us will be raised imperishable (see 1 Corinthians 15:42), but that doesn't mean we're discards. Quite the reverse. It means that the bodies we are born with are the only things God intends for us to use for just this lifetime. The physical body isn't just an earthly tent or a useful container but also a means of

God's revelation, a temple of the Holy Spirit, and a sanctuary of the living God. The love of Christ made this possible and the Holy Spirit makes it available to us.

So rather than deny, excuse, or tune out our bodies, we're meant to tune in to them—heart, soul, mind, and strength—for our good and for the good of our neighbors, as we put God's love into action. If God wants to be known fully and personally, how better than to speak to each of us through our lives as we live them? If the God who created us has set us on our course to completion, the commandment to love is our catalyst.

However, we must be vigilant. We know that not all movement is at God's direction. Hurriedness, busyness, and pushing ahead may easily take us off course, while our refusal or resistance may leave us stuck. How can we know whether we are moving at the invitation of God? The daily practice of devotional time with dedicated activities such as the those offered here in *Made to Move* can help.

Each of us learns to attend to the call of God day by day as we practice loving God with all that we are and loving our neighbor as ourselves. Though we may sometimes stumble and fall in our attempts to follow Jesus, even scraped knees can serve as a tangible reminder of the nearness of God. The evidence of our senses, the reasoning of our minds, the performance of our bodies—even the aching of our joints and the injury to our egos—can speak to us of God.

Each of us has a body, uniquely created and wonderfully made. We are made to move in God's direction, at God's command, by God's initiative, and at God's pace. Our bodies will speak to us if we listen. Our bodies will teach us if we pay attention. God made us this way. All living things are made to move. That is a defining characteristic of life itself. And if, as scripture promises, we are created in the image of God (see Genesis 1:26), then we know that God is on the move in us and among us, always.

In dedicating ourselves to this Made to Move journey, we let God tell us our own stories. No two will be alike as no two people are alike. Yet, the arc of our human story is so familiar: a body created in God's image is tempted, broken, yielded, rebuilt, and renewed. It's the story Christ lived, and still lives in us, so that through us God may be glorified, and others may come to know the hope of Christ that we have.

"From one ancestor he made all nations to inhabit the whole earth, and he allotted the times of their existence and the boundaries of the places where they would live, so that they would search for God and perhaps grope for him and find him—though indeed he is not far from each one of us. For 'In him we live and move and have our being'" (Acts 17:26-28).

Let's begin together in prayer: *Lord, use the workings of my body to show me the mysteries of my soul. Thank you for moving in me. Make me a willing participant in your ongoing work of creation, that I might claim the abundant life you offer. Amen.*

How to Use This Book

This book of daily devotional experiences is designed to help you understand yourself, that amazing puzzle that only you and God can solve together. Through scripture, meditation, reflection, activity, and prayer, the readings will guide you to fill out the image of God in you and bring living color to the masterpiece God made you to be.

Each week contains seven daily devotional read-and-respond pages, one for each day of the week. Our framework follows the Great Commandment, given by God to Moses for the people of Israel (see Deuteronomy 6:4-9) and by Jesus to the inquisitive scribe of the day (see Mark 12:28-31).

Monday through Friday we will consider what it means to love the Lord our God with heart, soul, mind, and strength, and to love our neighbor as ourselves. On Saturdays, we will address how loving obedience shapes us and orders our lives. On Sundays, we practice resting intentionally, and we claim rest and renewal for the rest of our week.

So, our days together will look like this:

- Sunday/Day 1—Rest and Renew
- Monday/Day 2—Heart
- Tuesday/Day 3—Soul
- Wednesday/Day 4—Mind
- Thursday/Day 5—Strength
- Friday/Day 6—Neighbor
- Saturday/Day 7—Order

Note: You or your group's schedule may wish to begin the study on a day other than Sunday. If so, it is perfectly fine to make Day 1 a different day of the week.

Each day we will read selected scripture, pray into our daily devotion, then engage with the activity for the day. Our day's theme will follow the pattern above with questions meant to help us reflect on our experience and guide us toward where God may be moving us.

Study Resources

Each participant will need the following:

- a copy of *Made to Move*
- a Bible or online Bible resource
- basic art supplies—e.g., colored pencils, crayons, markers, paper, etc.
- a simple movement space—a chair with arms, wall, floor with carpet or cushioning or yoga mat, outdoor walking/running/biking space
- an internet connection to access video demonstrations of activities
- group leader's guide for small groups (included at the end of this workbook)
- children's guide designed for Sunday school or weeknight meetings (included in this workbook)

Additional Resources

- resistance band(s) available in various "weights" for light, moderate, or heavy resistance, and with a latex-free option (see wendylebolt.com website or online vendors)
- basic exercise equipment (optional)—hand weights, yoga mat, rubber tubing, or fitness facility equipment

Since every human has a body, *Made to Move* is meant for everybody. Men and women, boys and girls of all ages, lifelong Christians and those new to the idea of faith—everyone is invited to join in the fun of finding God in your days through *Made to Move* activities. While this devotional workbook is designed to be used as part of a daily devotional time, it is my hope that you will join a small group (in person or online) to share your experience with others.

If you are part of a faith community, *Made to Move* is a perfect intergenerational Christian learning opportunity. Invite the whole congregation to do the workbook together!

- For children: Nothing is more natural to children than movement. They are born to move and excited to be active. The activities will help children discover how they're uniquely and wonderfully made by exploring how their bodies work by God's great design.
- For teens and students: Reading and reflecting on the miraculous nature of their bodies will invite students to appreciate the creative diversity in God's loving handiwork, which has formed each of them in God's image.

- For adults: Adults will enjoy the energy and fun of being active in their faith, even as they are inspired to find that inner child who used to turn somersaults and cartwheels in the backyard or shoot hoops in the driveway.
- For seniors: We never grow out of our bodies, minds, or souls. The wisdom, energy efficiency, perspective, and endurance provided by the seniors in our communities are the hallmarks of seniority. It's why we call seniors *elders*.

Together we are the complete expression of the body of Christ. Wholly and abundantly alive, learning, and growing, our bodies are designed to walk us through all the seasons of our lives. In our collective design we see the hand of the Great Designer.

Let's get going.

1

Body Image

For it was you who formed my inward parts;
    you knit me together in my mother's womb.
I praise you, for I am fearfully and wonderfully made.
    Wonderful are your works;
that I know very well.
    My frame was not hidden from you,
when I was being made in secret,
    intricately woven in the depths of the earth.
Your eyes beheld my unformed substance.
In your book were written
    all the days that were formed for me,
    when none of them as yet existed.

—Psalm 139:13-16

You are a unique creation of God's own design. This week, let us marvel at the hand of the designer who has brought you to life.

Sunday, Week 1

Created Not Constructed

Read Psalm 139:1-18.

> For it was you who formed my inward parts;
>   you knit me together in my mother's womb.
> I praise you, for I am fearfully and wonderfully made.
>   Wonderful are your works;
> that I know very well.
>
> —Psalm 139:13-14

G. K. Chesterton wrote, "The whole difference between construction and creation is exactly this: that a thing constructed can only be loved after it is constructed; but a thing created is loved before it exists."*

You were created. Take a moment to stand in front of the mirror and take a good look at yourself. Yes, you are what you see, but you are also what you don't see. You are everything that is inside that miraculous body standing before you; and God loves every inch of you. Hard to believe? Yes, perhaps because we have so much evidence to the contrary. We know there are so many places we fall short of answering the call to love God with our whole selves, to love God the way God loves us.

God knew this would happen. God knew we would forget. That's why God says to us, *You of poor memory, I will write this down for you. I will send a Savior to teach you. After that I will send an Advocate to remind you of all he has taught.* God knows we are

---

*G. K. Chesterton, *Appreciations and Criticisms of the Works of Charles Dickens* (New York: EP Dutton & Co, 1911), 14.

imperfect people—who knows us better than God does?—and yet God doesn't lower the standards but raises the expectations. God knows we can do this: God in us, us in God, in fellowship with each other.

Activity

- If you were a construction project, what would you look like? Use colored pencils, pens, crayons, or markers to draw yourself as a construction project.
- Imagine the day of your creation when you were knitted together in the womb. Draw yourself as a creation project, God's creation that is constituted in you.
- Overlay your drawings—creation over construction—and hold them up to the light. What do you see? What does love show you?

Reflection

- What does it mean to be created by God?
- What might that mean about the way you see yourself? Treat yourself? Care for yourself?
- What does this say about God?

Prayer

Creator God, the knowledge that you made me is too great for me and too much for me to understand. Yet, I am here. I live and breathe. My heart beats and my mind thinks. You loved me before I took my first breath. I am your expression of love, alive. Teach me to love in a way that loves you back. Amen.

Monday, Week 1

The Heartbeat of Life

Read Genesis 1:26-27.

> So God created humankind in his image, in the image of God he created them; male and female he created them.

—Genesis 1:27

I will never forget the moment that modern technology allowed me to hear that tiny new heart beating inside me for the first time. It was racing way faster than my own heartbeat, but regular and strong, giving me confidence that this newly conceived life was off to a healthy start. All of this at six weeks! Before anyone else knew my daughter was alive, I did. I had a real life growing inside of me. What a responsibility! Now, everything I did, I did for two.

The heart we grow up with began with God; it belongs to both of us. All that we do to, for, and with our bodies affects our hearts, which is both God's and ours. That which is done to us affects the heart too. God knew this before we were born. God knew that we would need an organ to circulate our life blood and that it would have to work hard, sometimes persevere against resistance, and above all, need a regular rhythm. There in our chest is the first sign of our life and an indicator of our health. The heart is an organ so sensitive that its heart-shaped symbol represents Valentine's Day love.

It is hard to conceive of love so great and so constant, but God gave us a perfect reminder in our own beating heart.

Activity

- Sit or lie still and put your hand over your heart. "Listen" through your hand to the sound of God's presence, beating in your depths. Give thanks for this constant presence and evidence of God's constancy in your life.

- Remain still and count the rhythmic beats of your heart for one minute. This, your resting heart rate, is the pace designed by God to serve your circulatory needs at rest.
- As your body allows, perform an activity that increases your heart rate. Climb the stairs, go for a walk or jog, or try a few simple calisthenics. After activity, count the beats again.
- Imagine the life-giving work your heart is doing both at rest and also with activity/ at work. Give thanks to God for the heart beating in you, which is both rhythmic and responsive.

Reflection

- How do you think God felt at the sound of your first heartbeat?
- What does the beating of your heart say about the image of God created in you?
- What does the speeding and slowing of your heart show you about your Creator?

Prayer

Creator God, how you formed the heart in me and started it beating is a mystery I may never fully understand, but its pulse is dutiful and constant. Remind me that it is a strong and sure sign of your presence with me through everything I do and in everything I need. Amen.

Tuesday, Week 1

The Breath of Life

Read Genesis 2:4-7.

> Then the LORD God formed man from the dust of the ground, and breathed into his nostrils the breath of life; and the man became a living being.
>
> —Genesis 2:7

In Hebrew, Greek, Latin, and English, the word *inspire* is connected to the breath that enters us from the outside and makes us alive. We may have a quick intake of breath when something startles us. We may take a deep breath when something astounds us. When majesty and awe overwhelm us, our breath pauses as we relish the moment of inspiration.

Our life's very first breath was an inhalation and probably not so inspiring. As a newborn, we cough and sputter as we try out those inspiratory muscles for the first time to inflate lungs that have never been filled with air before. In the womb our oxygen had always come in liquid form. The moment we breathe in gaseous air, we cry. Mothers often hear it as the sound of life. For our infant selves, it is more of a gasp. Babies delivered early sometimes need a ventilator to help them breathe until they can breathe for themselves.

Today's scripture from Genesis tells us that God forms the first man from the dust of the ground and that his first breath is breathed into him by his Creator, a supernatural ventilator! The lungs God had prepared expanded and contracted, made to breathe without thought. God designed us for respiration, rhythmic inhale and exhale, in and out. Life demands both.

Activity

- Close your eyes and slowly draw in a deep, deep breath. Feel your lungs inflating as your chest expands and abdomen rises. Hold it briefly, and then slowly expel the air from your lungs, compressing it and then letting it slip slowly out through your lips, emptying your airways. Listen to the air as you exhale it.
- Repeat this deep breathing. Inhale . . . 2, 3. Hold. Exhale . . . 2, 3.
- Try matching words of prayer to this breath. (Some suggestions—inhale: *Thanks be to God.* Exhale: *For the gift of life.* Or, *You in me . . . Me in thee.* Or, *Lord Jesus Christ . . . Have mercy on me.*)
- Write the words of your breath prayer on paper or a card to carry with you throughout the day. Any time you breathe, you can pray it. The breath is available to you as a reminder to pray, at all times and in all circumstances.

Reflection

- Breath prayer has been practiced throughout the ages, experienced as God breathing life into you and you breathing thanks back to God. How did the rhythm of your breath feel?

- Breath was God's first gift to your earthly life. Be inspired. Breathe deeply. What have you discovered or uncovered as you engaged in the practice of breath prayer?

Prayer

Giver of life, you inflated our lungs with air to breathe and brought us thus to life. You have provided for the cleansing and refreshing of air by the green plants you've given us for partnership and sustenance. Yet, it is not the air but the breath itself that is miraculous because you drew so near to deliver it. May I honor that first breath with all the others I take. Amen.

Wednesday, Week 1   *July 22*

The Reason of Life

Read Psalm 8.

> What are human beings that you are mindful of them,
>   mortals that you care for them?

—Psalm 8:4

Newly born, we are completely dependent on others not only to provide for our bodily needs and comforts but also for the stimulation of our growing minds. Our infant brain sends and receives a vast array of signals as it searches for what connects, sticks, and makes sense. Trial and error via the pattern and repetition that we experience in the world is our mind's first task. The work is both monumental and simple, and it is necessary in order to distinguish between what is me and what is not me. We learn to differentiate.

On the face of it, trial-and-error development seems random, even to those who study the brain. To think that God might leave this essential development to chance seems irresponsible or even unethical. We are born helpless, blank canvases upon which life paints its picture, trying out colors and mixing hues. Yet, for a God who paints a sunrise on the strength of three primary colors, is it really unreasonable to think that from the raw material of brain matter, God could grow magnificent minds?

Even conceiving of such a thing is mind-blowing! After all, the process of growing our minds and their thoughts is so detailed and tenuous that a signal gone even slightly askew could result in a cascade of messages gone awry. Such crafting of a human mind would require God's full attention over our lifetime. Yet "what are human beings that you are mindful of them, mortals that you care for them?" (Ps. 8:4). In the shaping of our minds, God never looks away.

Activity

- Do you have a memento or family heirloom that brings back a fond memory? Is it a photo? writing? artwork? letter? other memorabilia? Hold this memory item gently and reverently. Offer it in prayer.
- What does God want to show you or help you remember about this time in your life, this person, or this place?
- Animate this memory by journaling, sketching, dancing, singing, or otherwise responding to what God has shown you.
- Offer a prayer of thanks for God's guidance, insight, and safe passage through this time of remembering with you.

Reflection

- What does it mean that God is mindful of you?
- How does it feel to know that God is at work in your mind?
- What would you like to share with God? Hold that thought gently with God and imagine communication traveling between you in both directions.

Prayer

I was but an unformed thought in your mind when I was conceived. Day after day, this idea is being realized in the life you gave me. Born a babe in the wilderness of the world, you gave me the capacity to know and to understand. Lord, guide me toward your wisdom. Incline my mind and shape my thoughts that they might be centered on you alone. Amen.

Thursday, Week 1

The Strength of Life

Read Psalm 31.

> Be strong, and let your heart take courage,
>   all you who hope in the LORD.
>
> —Psalm 31:24

There are all kinds of strengths. I wonder if God had this in mind in creating the diversity of body types among us: thin, thicker, and thickest. The psalmist encourages all of us, regardless of muscle mass, to take heart and be strong.

We don't get to pick our body type; we just accept our assignment as God's gift and do our best to work with it. Regardless of our portion in the distribution, we're meant to be strong. The naturally muscular (mesomorphs) may do the heavy lifting with ease, but God assures us that the endomorphs (thicker ones) and ectomorphs (thinner ones) are fearfully and wonderfully made too. Wiry strength and curvy contours are perfectly acceptable expressions of God's strong design; they're just packaged differently.

Activity

- What is your body type? Use a whole sheet of paper to make a simple line drawing of the outline of your body.
- Where has God made you strong? (Head, shoulders, knees, toes, hands, heart, gut, etc.) Shade in those places. Where has God shown you a weakness? Circle this or these.
- Make a fist and flex your arm muscles. Holding the tension, draw your hand toward your shoulder (exercise known as a bicep curl) and notice the muscles that are working, contracting to allow you to move. Picture God's amazing design for your body in motion.

- As you go through your day, use your body with intention. As you sit, stand, lift, carry, hold, or otherwise use your body to move, consider the miracle of design that makes this possible.

Reflection

- What part(s) of you has God made strong? What kind of strength or fortitude has God invested in you? How will you use this strength?
- What part(s) of you need God's strengthening? Ask God for strength in this weakness. How might God make you stronger?
- Pray this prayer of praise to God: "For it was you who formed my inward parts; you knit me together in my mother's womb. I praise you, for I am fearfully and wonderfully made. Wonderful are your works; that I know very well" (Ps. 139:13-14).

Prayer

Thank you for making me and loving me as I am. My unique composition is exactly what you intended. Satisfy me with that and show me the strong places in me along with the ones that need strengthening. Draw these places together just as you knit me together fearfully, wonderfully, and perfectly. In the strong name of Jesus, I pray. Amen.

Friday, Week 1

The Reach of Life

Read Genesis 1:28–2:1.

> God blessed them, and God said to them, "Be fruitful and multiply, and fill the earth and subdue it; and have dominion over the fish of the sea and over the birds of the air and over every living thing that moves upon the earth."
>
> —Genesis 1:28

What is our purpose here on earth? Why are we here? The human brain has a tough time wrapping itself around those big questions. It is natural to look around for suggestions and within ourselves for answers. Who does the world tell me I am? What does the world tell me I should be?

A generous God has provided the earth and everything in it to help us with these questions. I imagine God seems to say, *"Go ahead. Here is your playground. Go play in it!"* While the playground helps us stay healthy, it also teaches us how to get along with others. We learn to wait our turn and how to play fairly. Our interactions with others on the playground, while sometimes boisterous, can help develop skills for more than recess. We discover what we like and what we're good at. We're also meant to learn how to work together. It's everybody's playground.

More than simply satisfied with the work of creation God completed on the sixth day, God proclaimed it *very* good, then entrusted it to us. That's an awesome task and a huge responsibility, sure to stretch us to our *very* limit. But in our working for the good of all creation, we set about finding answers to our biggest questions—not only why we're here but also what we're here to do. Tending to and caring for creation is a job way bigger than any one of us. We had better reach to join hands.

Activity

- How flexible are you? From a sitting position, with legs as straight as you can get them, gently bend forward toward your toes. Can you reach them? If not, it's okay! For assistance, you can loop a towel, band, or a short length of rope under your feet to gently pull yourself forward. (See https://upperroombooks.com/madetomove.)
- Reach for your toes, close your eyes, and hold your stretch. Inhale and exhale, relaxing the muscles in the backs of your legs. Check in with all body parts to see how they feel. Are you tempted to pull yourself forward? Be gentle. Resist the urge to force the stretch.
- Wiggle your toes. Point and flex them. Smile at the silliness of it. Can you bend a bit further without pain or discomfort? Go ahead. Close your eyes. Check in again.
- Sit up tall and give thanks to God for your flexibility in whatever state you find it and for God's willingness to stretch you.

Reflection

- How did it feel to stretch? If we haven't stretched in a while, our bodies know. Regular, gradual stretching improves our flexibility. It helps us reach farther and feel better.

- Were you tempted to force the stretch farther than was comfortable? Were you surprised at how short your reach was? Or happy with how far you could go?
- What in your life feels inflexible right now? How could you extend your life-reach without forcing the stretch?

Prayer

God of heaven and earth, thank you for reaching down to us with your hand of grace. You have been flexible with us, offering us mercy we don't deserve and forgiveness we have not earned. In our gratitude, help us to extend our reach to those in need around us. Develop our flexibility, we pray, stretching us beyond what is comfortable toward more than we could ever imagine. Amen.

Saturday, Week 1

Bounded: The Guardrails of Life

Read Psalm 23.

> He makes me lie down in green pastures;
>   leads me beside still waters;
>   he restores my soul.
>
> He leads me in right paths
>   for his name's sake.
>
> —Psalm 23:4

We are gifted with a life all our own. What a privilege it is to spend it however we wish, but what a tremendous responsibility. When I think about the treasure God says that I am, and as I consider the ways God is present with me, I am in complete awe and full-blown fear. What if I mess this up?

God our Good Shepherd has foreseen what might befall us and, in the familiar words of Psalm 23, promises to be with us through it all. Unfortunately, God doesn't run interference for us. God walks with us through it, not over or around it. Imagine God assuring you, *"Life will go better for you, if you stick with me. Have I ever steered you wrong? Do what I tell you, follow the rules, apply yourself completely, and stay on the straight and narrow. Trust me and all will go well."*

The life of faith looks beautiful and easy from a distance, but it can feel very confining up close. So many rules. So many prohibitions. So many boundaries. But the guardrails God provides are meant to prevent us from experiencing the harshest of consequences during our early learning. Our persistence will pay off if we trust our Shepherd and don't get to wandering. Mature faith is set free to embrace the beauty that was once in the distance, free of the fear of falling.

Activity

- Read Psalm 23 aloud slowly.
- Pray this prayer before reading the psalm a second time: *Dear Lord, open my heart and mind to the power of your Word, that as I read, I may know, understand, and obey your word for me today.* Receive with thanks what God opens to you as you read Psalm 23 in prayer.
- Write a response. Copy the verses of Psalm 23 and then, in an attitude of prayer, respond in your own way. Use written words, movement, music, images, colors, or another form of personal expression to enhance and claim your response.
- You may wish to close your prayer time today by reading the new version of Psalm 23 that you revised with God's help.

Reflection

- How did it feel to respond to this psalm?
- Were you surprised? challenged? affirmed? reminded? convicted? renewed?
- What did God reveal to you in this exercise about yourself? about God? about your journey of faith? Give thanks for the insight God has provided.

Prayer

Dear Lord, open my heart and mind to the power of your Word, that as I go about my day, I may know, understand, and obey your word for me. I pray this, trusting in Jesus' name. Amen.

2

Body of Flesh

Jesus, full of the Holy Spirit, returned from the Jordan and was led by the Spirit in the wilderness, where for forty days he was tempted by the devil. He ate nothing at all during those days, and when they were over, he was famished.

—Luke 4:1-2

Jesus, the Son of God, was fully God and fully human. He knew temptation. This week, let us admit that, in our humanity, we are subject to temptation.

Sunday, Week 2

We the Temple

Read 1 Corinthians 6:12-20.

> Or do you not know that your body is a temple of the Holy Spirit within you, which you have from God, and that you are not your own? For you were bought with a price; therefore glorify God in your body.
>
> —1 Corinthians 6:19-20

What do you have that you couldn't bear to lose? Asked another way, if your home caught on fire, what would be the one thing you would take with you? To what lengths would you go to be sure it got out safely? Oh, how we protect what is precious.

I once went to the National Archives building in Washington, DC, where our nation houses its most treasured documents. The original copies of the Declaration of Independence, the Constitution of the United States, and the Bill of Rights are on exhibit. They are carefully kept under glare-resistant, shatterproof glass so people can file by to view them but not touch them. These documents are so carefully guarded because they are originals.

You are an original. Nothing exists anywhere else in the world quite like your person or your life. God hasn't placed you behind shatterproof glass, rather God has formed you in flesh because you're not just for display; you are alive. Living will expose you to wear and tear and the risk of potential harm or injury. Still, God pours the Holy Spirit into our human form—breakable, bendable, flesh though it is. You were bought with a price. You are precious to God.

Activity

- Place your palms flat against each other and assume the posture of prayer. Rub your palms together or fold them to interlocking, flesh against flesh. Bow your head in thanks to God for the sensation of touch.
- With your eyes closed, extend your prayer. Wrap your arms around yourself in a hug, thanking God for your body. Then releasing the hug, draw your hands along your body, touching shoulders, then arms, then hands. Move to head, face, neck, chest, torso, abdomen, hips, thighs, legs, feet. Are there sensitive places? Injured? Healing? Treat them with special care.
- During the day, notice how you tend to and care for the outside (the protective covering) of your body: brushing, washing, trimming, drying, powdering, beautifying, anointing with fragrance, moisturizing, protecting with sunblock, etc.

Reflection

- Skin is a guardian of our body—a sentry of sorts—meant to protect the temple of our body. When skin is healthy, not much gets through it. How much time do you spend caring for your outsides (skin, hair, nails, etc.)? Is that care intended for health, appearance, or both? Is the time you spend tending to your outer self too little, too much, or about right?
- Skin is also sensitive and specially designed to signal a range of sensations from sweet caress to potential danger. Where is your skin especially sensitive? Less sensitive? Why do you think that is?
- Scripture says that "your body is a temple of the Holy Spirit within you" (1 Cor. 6:19), not built of stone and mortar, but created of flesh and blood. If the Spirit resides in you, what can you do to honor the gift of life in your body?

Prayer

Holy Spirit, come. You give life to my inner being. Teach me how to let that show from the inside out. Let my very flesh be a reminder that I am covered in your love. Let me give off such effervescence that all who see me know I am alive in you. Amen.

Monday, Week 2

Heart Grab

Read Romans 7:15-20.

> For I have the desire to do what is good, but I cannot carry it out. For I do not do the good I want to do, but the evil I do not want to do—this I keep on doing.
>
> —Romans 7:18-19 (NIV)

I'm only human! How often I want to shout this when the world around me tantalizes and tempts. *Don't you want this? Wouldn't you like to join that? This would be good to do, good to have. You know you want it. It will make you happy!* I deserve to be happy, don't I? Before I know it, I have a life full of things I hadn't bargained for that all promised to make life easier. Instead, they have made things much, much more complicated.

Ah, the heart of humankind, deceitful above all things. (See Jeremiah 17:9.) The world says follow your heart, dream your dreams, and pursue your passion. But somehow the world slips itself in as the answer to our longings and the fulfillment of our dreams, distracting and deceiving us. It wants us to skip to the satisfaction rather than forge our way through the valley of discontent meant to teach us how to be content along the way.

Thank goodness for the apostle Paul's admission in Romans 7. He understood what we would go through because he lamented just as we lament. "For I have the desire to do what is good, but I cannot carry it out. For I do not do the good I want to do, but the evil I do not want to do—this I keep on doing" (Rom. 7:18-19, NIV). Yet Paul persisted. His human nature exhausted him, but there was more to Paul than that. There is more to us too.

Activity

- What's the best activity for you? It's the one that fills you and leaves you with more energy and satisfaction. On cards or small pieces of paper, write five to ten "heart healthy" things you would be willing to do for ten to twenty minutes of your day. Examples: take a walk, ride a bike, jump rope, climb stairs, jog, plan a healthy meal, play with a child, call a good friend, write in your journal, send an encouraging note. Be creative; God knows what is healthy for your heart.
- Fold the papers and put them in a hat, jar, or container where you can easily draw one out at random. This is your heart grab bag.
- Choose one activity from the grab bag and do it today. Dedicate the time and effort to God and see what God shows you in the doing.

Reflection

- How did it feel to come up with heart-healthy activities? Was that exercise easy or difficult for you to do? If you struggled with it, what made the task difficult?
- In choosing from the grab bag, did you hope you would get a particular activity? If you didn't pull that one out, did you do it anyway? Why or why not?
- What did God show you in this exercise? In creating the options? In the performing of the activity?

Prayer

Loving God, you know my heart better than I know it myself. You know my tendency to let it lead me or maybe deceive me. When I let you lead me, you never deceive me. You guide me toward what is good, for me and for those around me. Help me follow wholeheartedly. Amen.

Tuesday, Week 2

Daily Bread: Our Portion

Read Luke 4:1-13.

> Jesus answered him, "It is written, 'One does not live by bread alone.'"
>
> —Luke 4:4

Imagine Jesus, fresh from his baptism in the Jordan and full of the Holy Spirit, when the Spirit led him into the wilderness, where he stayed for forty days and ate nothing. He was famished, Luke tells us. Oh, and the devil was there.

Temptation seems to know when we are at our weakest. It is clever too. It doesn't just serve what we want on a platter; we're too smart for that. It twists our desire into something that looks like a good thing. Food, prosperity, safety—surely God wouldn't deny me these? My soul says no, but my flesh says otherwise: maybe if I wait a while, it will stop knocking, stop asking, and stop tempting. No, seeing it has us weakening. Yet, temptation usually sweetens the deal: "Come on. I'll throw in tickets to the game, free wifi, and a buffet breakfast. What are you waiting for?"

That's when it's time for a soul check. Is this bread to me? Will it satisfy? If it hadn't been so long since I'd eaten, would I be saying yes to this? Temptation doesn't go away of its own accord. It must be sent. Each of us is tempted as Jesus was, so we're in good company. But God has shown us what is good for us. "It is written, 'One does not live by bread alone'" (Luke 4:4).

Activity

- Read Matthew 6:9-13 (the Lord's Prayer).
- Pray as the Lord taught us to pray . . .
    Our Father in heaven, hallowed be your name,

your kingdom come, your will be done,
    on earth as it is in heaven.
Give us today our daily bread.
And forgive us our debts,
    as we also have forgiven our debtors.
And lead us not into temptation,
    but deliver us from the evil one.

- Hold out your hands as you repeat the italicized verse: *Give us today our daily bread.* Slowly repeat this verse as you emphasize a different word on each succeeding repetition.

    Give *us today our daily bread.*
    Give **us** *today our daily bread.*
    Give us **today** *our daily bread.*
    Give us today **our** *daily bread.*
    Give us today our **daily** *bread.*
    Give us today our daily **bread***.*

- Commit to using whatever God puts in your hands today in the way God has shown you.

Reflection

- What is "daily bread" to you?
- What is the portion God delivers to you daily?
- Are you tempted to ask for more? to doubt that there is enough? Why?

Prayer

Generous Lord, I know you are always enough, but I have a hard time trusting this. Remind me that when I am tempted, you will deliver me if I ask. You are what I need. You will not leave me hungry. Forgive me for doubting you, Lord. Amen.

Wednesday, Week 2

Stuck in My Head

Read 2 Samuel 11:1-27.

> One evening David got up from his bed and walked around on the roof of the palace. From the roof he saw a woman bathing. The woman was very beautiful, and David sent someone to find out about her.
>
> —2 Samuel 11:2-3 (NIV)

At first, it's just a harmless thought. She's beautiful; beauty is God-given. There is nothing wrong with appreciating, or even admiring, beauty. But David can't take his eyes off this woman bathing. He is intrigued, and his interest is piqued. *Is she available? I am the king; I can inquire. She's another man's wife? No problem, the man is off at battle. What are her thoughts? What might she want or not want? It doesn't matter. Bring her to me.*

Scripture warns us that, "anyone who looks at a woman lustfully has already committed adultery with her in his heart" (Matt. 5:28). God knows our minds and how feeble we are to resist what we let ourselves think about. Too easily, idea gives birth to action, and sin conceives.

All of us are tempted by something, just as the fully human Jesus was tempted in the desert. Also fully divine, he resisted. We spend our lives in that battle, trying mightily to resist the thing that seems to keep heading straight for us like a heat-seeking missile. Where is our willpower to decline what we know isn't good for us? How can we separate ourselves from what we know has the power to separate us from our Lord?

Whatever tempts us, we can address it to God, who knows what we're thinking anyway. We will find help to turn from temptation as we turn to God in prayer. "Not my will, but yours be done."

Activity

- Begin listening to or singing a song you enjoy. Stop abruptly in the middle of the song. Does it keep playing in your head? (That's called an earworm.)
- Start the song again at the beginning, but this time, play, listen, and sing it all the way through to the end. Is your earworm gone or does the song continue to play in your mind?
- During the day today, pay special attention to the thoughts playing in your head, especially the ones that keep repeating. Do you speak them? Act on them? Keep them to yourself?
- Is there a soundtrack that doesn't belong? Offer this to God. Repeat as needed.

Reflection

- How did it feel to tune in to your thought soundtrack?
- What song is currently stuck in your head or playing out in your life?
- If you played the current rendition to its conclusion, how would it end?
- What plans are you making with God to rework your soundtrack?

Prayer

O God, my life is an open book to you. Yet I hide, pretending you won't see or won't notice what I do that disappoints you. I want to live a life that makes you smile with approval. Help me be honest with myself and with you. Help me acknowledge what comes between us so we can work on it together. I love you, Lord. Thank you for loving me. Amen.

Thursday, Week 2

In My Own Strength

Read 2 Corinthians 12:7-10.

That is why, for Christ's sake, I delight in weaknesses, in insults, in hardships, in persecutions, in difficulties. For when I am weak, then I am strong.

—2 Corinthians 12:10 (NIV)

We feel best about ourselves when we operate in our strengths, choosing to do what we're good at while leaving the rest for others. There's nothing wrong with being strong. Fortitude and perseverance get things done. Strength is respected and admired, often aspired to and imitated.

I'm grateful for a study group partner who once admonished, "Sometimes it's our strengths that pose the most risk." If we're not careful, strengths can become strongholds of our own making. In confident self-reliance, we whisk God away to go help someone who really needs the help. There, in our "strong" places, we may find ourselves particularly exposed and unprotected because we have put our trust in ourselves.

God gives each of us gifts that God expects us to use to build up the kingdom, but we're not meant to use them without God. In our own strength, we may go very far in our own direction before we realize how far off course we've gone. Then, to bring us back, God must exert a mighty effort to reel us in or, as with Paul, set a thorn in our flesh that God refuses to take away. Brought down to size, we have no choice but to look up. Now God's got our attention.

Activity

(See https://upperroombooks.com/madetomove.)

- Basic option: Balance on one foot (without holding on, if you can) and see how long you can stand without falling. Try the other foot. For a challenge, repeat your effort with your eyes closed. (Have a handhold ready to steady you.) Record your best time for each attempt on each foot.
- Advanced option: Try a one-legged squat. Standing on one foot with arms out and head up, bend at the knee while continuing to keep your balance. (Caution: Sink the hips back as if sitting in a chair. Prevent the bent knee from going further forward than your big toe.) How low can you go comfortably and safely? Try right and left, eyes open and eyes closed. Practice a few times to see if your balance improves. (Coaching cue: Try tightening the muscles of your abdomen to stabilize your torso when you balance.)
- On which foot was your balance better? Under which conditions was your balance better (eyes open or eyes closed)? Did having a handhold available help you balance even if you didn't hold on?

Reflection

- Which kind of balancing was easier, straight legged or bent knee? Right or left leg? Did practice help? What did you try that improved your balance? Why do you think it helped?
- Is one leg better at balancing than the other? Is one leg stronger than the other? Do you think strength and balance are related?
- What is the difference between your strength and God's strength? Does God's strength change? Does yours? Can yours? Can God's?

Prayer

Mighty God, you are all-powerful and yet so restrained. You allow us to fail and to fall and even to boast in our own strength. What strength it must require not to constantly correct us! Thank you for your patience. Right us. Balance us. Humble us before you that we may stand. Amen.

8-12-19

Friday, Week 2

And Who Is My Neighbor?

Read Luke 10:25-29, 30-37.

> Just then a lawyer stood up to test Jesus. "Teacher," he said, "what must I do to inherit eternal life?" He said to him, "What is written in the law? What do you read there?" He answered, "You shall love the Lord your God with all your heart, and with all your soul, and with all your strength, and with all your mind; and your neighbor as yourself." And he said to him, "You have given the right answer; do this, and you will live."
>
> But wanting to justify himself, he asked Jesus, "And who is my neighbor?"
>
> —Luke 10:25-29

"Officer, I can explain . . ."

We are full of reasons why we were doing what we were doing when we are caught doing what we shouldn't. The temptation to put ourselves in the right, to justify ourselves in order to assure our innocence, is strong. The expert in the law who stood up to test Jesus knew and practiced Jewish law to the letter, but he wanted to justify himself. *Teacher, just so we understand each other, who qualifies as my neighbor?*

As if loving God with our complete heart, soul, mind, and strength isn't hard enough, there's more. That neighbor—who doesn't look like me, sound like me, pray like me; who doesn't give me the time of day, and if we're being totally honest, whom I really don't like— I'm supposed to love him or her too.

It's not enough just to say so; we have to do it. It's not enough just to answer correctly on the true/false and multiple-choice questions; we have to get the essay question right too. What would our score be on this kind of test? Loving our neighbors is the life application portion of the class, where we put into practice what we've been taught. It shows if we have actually learned the lesson.

Who is *my* neighbor? The one who is stripped, beaten, and left for dead. Who *was the* neighbor? The one who showed mercy. Without mercy, the law of God is meaningless in our lives.

Activity

- Consider an ice skater or ballerina performing a spin. When they pull their arms and legs inward, they turn faster and faster. When they extend them again, they slow gracefully.
- Have you ever spun yourself in a circle and felt so dizzy when you stopped you fell down? Why doesn't the skater (or ballerina) fall? They don't get dizzy because they have mastered the art of "spotting." Each time around, they find a spot to look at that orients them.
- Turning in a narrow circle makes you dizzy. Extending your arms may slow you enough to keep your focus. For a challenge, try turning in a circle and see if you can look at one spot to keep your balance. Spins are for experts (and children who love feeling dizzy and have no fear of falling), so do this exercise carefully.

Reflection

- If you tried the challenge, how did it feel to spin? Were you dizzy? Did spotting help?
- What is your spot or focus in life? Can you spot God? What keeps you centered on God?
- Life today can move very fast and sometimes leave us spinning. What might slow you down? Would extending your arms help? What about reaching out to your neighbor?

Prayer

Teacher, your presence with me is all the assurance I should ever need, yet often I fail to turn to you for that assurance. And after failing, I often resort to explanations and excuses. Thank you for declining my excuses and inviting the better me to stand up. Help me live a life that holds its arms out, its head high, and you highest. Amen.

Saturday, Week 2

What Is Good Enough for God?

Read Micah 6:6-8.

> [God] has told you, O mortal, what is good;
>   and what does the LORD require of you
> but to do justice, and to love kindness,
>   and to walk humbly with your God?
>
> —Micah 6:8

The church sign reads, "Help wanted. Perfect people need not apply." I am certainly qualified for that position, but what is the job description? What are the expectations? Am I a good fit for the position they are advertising? Is what I have to offer what they are looking for? When my performance comes up for review, I want to be sure to measure up.

Life is so much more than a job. After all, this is God I am serving. I want to bring the perfect gift. I want to live a perfect life for the One who made me, but I fall so far short. The smallest distractions can take me off on a tangent or lead me astray. Before I know it, I have lost sight of the path the Lord and I had set out on together.

Somehow, God knows this because God knows us. Mercifully, God boils it down to the basics. "[God] has told you, O mortal, what is good; and what does the LORD require of you but to do justice, and to love kindness, and to walk humbly with your God?" (Mic. 6:8). These instructions sound perfectly reasonable, and yet they can seem completely impossible. God knows this too, that we are mere mortals. Perfect people need not apply. We're hired. Now let's get to work.

Activity

- How is your posture? Stand with your heels against the base of a wall. With your abdomen held tight, press your hips back against the wall, then your shoulder blades and finally the back of your head. Remain in this position for a count of thirty. Breathe slowly and deeply.
- Maintaining your "wall" posture, take a step away from the wall. Does this posture feel strange to you? How does it feel compared to your normal posture? Step back against the wall to see how well you have maintained your "perfect posture."
- Transfer your good posture to a seated position. Sit toward the front of a sturdy chair that allows you to place your feet flat on the floor with knees bent at a ninety-degree angle. Can you stay in this posture while doing your seated activities?

Reflection

- What is your normal life posture? Head down? Buried in work/book/screen/other? Head up? Watching out? Looking around? Waiting? Ready? Looking straight ahead?
- What does your life posture say about you? What would you like your posture to tell other people about you?
- What might you do to maintain a posture of uprightness?

Prayer

Loving God, I'm reluctant to come before you with my meager offering. Yet knowing you are both merciful and just gives me courage. Humbled, I come before you to put all I have at your disposal. Use it for your glory. Amen and amen.

3

Body Broken

The LORD is near to the brokenhearted,
  and saves the crushed in spirit.

—Psalm 34:18

Why are you cast down, O my soul,
  and why are you disquieted within me?
Hope in God; for I shall again praise him,
  my help and my God.

—Psalm 42:11

Much in this world leaves us feeling downcast and brokenhearted. This week let us consider how God can lift us up to contend with a broken world.

Sunday, Week 3

This Way Out

Read 1 Corinthians 10:1-13.

> No testing has overtaken you that is not common to everyone. God is faithful, and he will not let you be tested beyond your strength, but with the testing he will also provide the way out so that you may be able to endure it.
>
> —1 Corinthians 10:13

"Don't worry. God won't give us more than we can handle."

We hear this kind of reassurance from others when life seems more than we can manage. If significant trials have caused us or those we love to suffer, we may have rejected the suggestion or at least wondered if God has overestimated our abilities. (The scripture frequently paraphrased or misquoted here is 1 Corinthians 10:13. Difficult problems are rarely solved by paraphrasing an incomplete scripture passage, no matter how sympathetic the tone.)

God doesn't promise that temptation and trouble won't come our way. In fact, Jesus assures us that in this world we will have trouble. (See John 16:33, NIV). Sometimes life's struggles can feel unbearable, unmanageable, and even unending. At such times God can seem distant and oh-so silent. Especially then it becomes tempting to rely only on ourselves or our own resources, figuring that God may be testing us.

God doesn't put us to the test. God takes us through the test. There is something about the fire of tribulation that melts and molds us into shapes of God's own design. Humankind is malleable, but God is constant and ever faithful. Were it not for the sharpening of our attention in the trial, perhaps we might never have noticed the exit sign flashing "THIS WAY!"

Activity

- Bend your elbows and cup your hands in a posture to receive as you would to receive the bread of communion. What do you bring? What, already, do you hold in your hands?
- Notice the bend in your elbows, the shape of your hands, and the arrangement of your fingers and thumbs. Consider what this design allows you to do. Make a list of these uses. (Suggestions: eat, drink, cover your mouth, blow a kiss, fold hands in prayer.)
- Now kneel or sit with knees bent, assuming a posture to receive. Notice which way your knees bend. (Hint: It is different from our elbows and different from most other animals.) How does kneeling or bending affect your perspective?
- Find a quiet place to pray. Give thanks to God for a body designed to assume a posture of prayer. Offer God thanks for the privilege of prayer.

Reflection

- It is unique to primates, including humans, that our elbows and shoulders bend forward, and our knees bend backward. Our ability to bend allows us not only to lift and reach but also to kneel and stand. This distinguishes us from other animals who "kneel" on their elbows when burdened. Why do you think God made us this way?
- Things bent under a weight may risk breaking. Is there something that feels broken to you? in you? What needs fixing? Offer this to God.
- What has been mended in you or perhaps just works differently than it used to? Thank God for this. What new wholeness may God be designing for you?

Prayer

God, sometimes it feels like I am Army-crawling through life. Under barbwire, through the mud, dodging bullets, and ducking enemy fire. Even when I see no way out, you have provided one. Show me the way through. Help me learn to trust you in life's toughest places. Amen.

8|9

Monday, Week 3

Heartbroken

Read Proverbs 3:1-4.

> My child, do not forget my teaching,
>> but let your heart keep my commandments.

—Proverbs 3:1

My father lay in the cardiac care unit, prepped for bypass surgery; and I knelt hundreds of miles away, weeping tears of hope and hopelessness. His heart was not strong, and I knew it. His body was not well maintained, and I knew it. Yet, they would be suspending that beating heart to reroute its blood flow in the hope of saving his life. Would he survive? I didn't know.

How I prayed for the life of this man, for this procedure, and for the surgeons who would perform it. I did not know them, but how well I knew him! A life of drink and smoke, coupled with inactivity and high-stress living, diminished his odds. Dad would tell you he'd been saved, but he had never called on the Lord in my hearing; so I called on the Lord for him. I didn't get far with words. God sent me an image from a surgery I once had. The surgeon signed my right leg in indelible marker, so he wouldn't operate on the wrong one. *Dear Daughter*, God seemed to say, *I have put my signature on your father's heart, in my own hand. He is mine. Trust in me.*

Later I learned that Dad's heart actually stopped beating during that bypass procedure, and the quick, capable hands of the surgical team revived him. Had he not been in the operating room, he would have surely perished. On December 11, 2008, he was quite literally given a new life, and I was given a renewed life with him. My earthly father and I were given five and a half more years together to grow in powerful relationship, thanks to the capable surgical hands that attended to him and the holy hands that held him that day and ushered him into all his days thereafter.

Activity

- Return to the heart grab bag you created last week, pull out all your options, and lay them in front of you. Are you still willing to do each of these heart-healthy things? If there is something you know you won't do, discard it. Write down other choices you would like to include and place them all back in the grab bag.
- Choose something from your refreshed grab bag. Note in a few words how you feel about doing it. Do it! Note in a few words how you feel after completing the activity.
- What did you choose? How did doing it change how you feel? Is this a feeling you want to hold onto? Name that feeling _____.

Reflection

- How do you feel about your grab bag? (Friendly, compelled, inclined, grateful, dutiful, forced, other?) Why?
- How is the grab bag motivating for you? Would you freely choose to be active without this motivation? If yes, why? If no, does the grab bag help? What does this add?
- Living life in a healthy and active way is good for your body and especially good for your heart. It's a way you can thank God for the heart God created in you. Have you ever thought of caretaking of your body as a matter of stewardship? Would thinking of it this way change your attitude or motivation toward how you live or approach healthy living?
- Give thanks to God for the heart that is in you. God has signed it and claimed you.

Prayer

Living God, life can be heartbreaking and heart-taking. Our hearts are fragile and sensitive to the day's events and the circumstances of life. Help us to trust that, even if life's hardships feel hard to overcome, you are both victor and healer. Lord of Life, you have signed our hearts and claimed our souls. In gratitude, help us to live every day growing in relationship with you and trusting your promise for the days to come. Amen.

Tuesday, Week 3

Gut Punch

Read Psalm 39.

> You have made my days a few handbreadths,
>   and my lifetime is as nothing in your sight.
> Surely everyone stands as a mere breath.

—Psalm 39:5

Huffing and puffing my way up the hill, I ran with the throng of my compatriots, working our way toward the 10k finish line. *Strong and steady,* I told myself. *One foot in front of the other.* Everything was going according to plan until I heard the hollow clang of a cowbell in the distance. As I came closer, I saw a solitary woman in her wheelchair, smiling and ringing her genuine encouragement. Her sincere offering touched me so deeply, it literally took my breath away. Unprepared for this, I had to walk until I could run again.

Plenty of moments in life leave us gasping for air. The gut punch of bad news, the crushing weight of tragedy or loss, the progression of illness, or the exasperation of unrelenting daily toil leave us breathless. Even a harsh word flung in our direction can feel like a direct blow, making it hard to breathe.

God knows that our moments spent gasping for air can be incapacitating and may leave us feeling faint. Our amazing Designer has anticipated such moments, programming into us a switch of sorts in the inspiratory center of our brains. Fainting flips the switch; without thinking, we breathe! God has thought of everything.

So when life lands a punch and it feels difficult to draw breath, God says, *Breathe. Breathe deeply in me.* It is as if God whispers, *Let go and let me take you up that hill to the finish line.*

Activity

- Sit in a relaxed position. Breathe in deeply, expanding your lungs, chest, and abdomen; and then release the breath, forcefully expelling the air from your lungs and airways. During Week 1, we discovered this can be a cleansing breath, preparing us to receive.
- Now, hold your breath. Count the seconds it takes before you need to breathe again. Don't hold it too long! Release your breath and sit quietly to let your breath regulate itself again. Is it more difficult to calm your breathing than before?
- Now, blow out several quick, short breaths as if you're exasperated with something that just occurred. Hold your breath again and count the seconds until you have to breathe. Did you last longer? (That's the fail-safe effect of your God-designed inspiratory center.)
- During your day, pay special attention to the pattern of your breath. Does it tend to be regular? deep? shallow? forced? exasperated? Make note of it. In times of tension or shortness of breath, call on God's breath to calm you.
- Special activity: If you have access to a labyrinth, monitor your breath as you walk it. Record your thoughts and insights.

Reflection

- Were you able to direct and calm your breath today? If yes, how did it feel? If no, what got in the way?
- Wherever you go, you take your breath with you. What does your breath suggest to you about the state of your body, mind, and spirit?
- Breathing in fresh air and breathing out stale air is essential to life. God programmed this into our subconscious design. Whether we are asleep, exhausted, emotionally spent, or overjoyed, we cannot forget to breathe. We read in Psalm 39 that our lives are but a breath. Even if, as the psalmist writes, *everyone stands as a mere breath*, what does that say about our God?

Prayer

Holy Spirit, come. I am growing short of breath. I try to breathe deeply, but shallow breaths are all I can muster. Reach deep inside me and fill me with your presence. Heal any heartache and quench my sadness. Breathe in me and restore me to your steady rhythm. More of you. Less of me. M-o-r-e. L-e-s-s. M-o-r-e. You. Amen.

Wednesday, Week 3

Shedding Light on Truth

Read John 18:33-38.

> Pilate asked [Jesus], "What is truth?"
>
> —John 18:38

"What is truth?" What a question! Can we trust the evidence of our eyes? The touch of our hands? The testimony of our heart and soul? When we struggle under the weight of unbearable sorrow, terrible news, interminable hardship, or persistent anguish, we grasp for something solid to hold on to. What is the truth here? Where can I find purchase, a ledge to stand on, or even a place to kneel? When my world is spinning out of control, I'm not sure which way is up. Am I out of my mind?

I will never forget sending out the plea over email airwaves asking for prayer for my high schooler who was in desperate need of God's protection in a meeting that was to take place at 3:00 p.m. I could not reach her, nor could I be there with her. I did not know what would happen. All I knew was my love for her and my desperation. A dear friend responded, "I will be on my knees for your daughter at 3:00 p.m."

How prayer changes us, even if it's someone else's prayer. When we can turn over to God what is beyond us, the weight lifts and peace enters. In that peace, new opportunity may present itself. A door may open that we would swear wasn't there a moment before. Such is the agility of a God-directed mind: what had been overrun by fear is now tamed by grace.

The light of God's love casts out fear. When, by prayers of petition and intercession, we open windows to let that light in, we can see differently and think more clearly. Suddenly, I see a resolution I hadn't even considered, and it's perfect. Why didn't I think of that before?

Activity

- Option 1: Prayer walk. Take your cares and concerns on a prayer walk. Read, think, and pray about a situation that has filled your mind with concern, then offer it to God as you head out to a street, trail, track, or other walking location. Release the situation to God and see what truth God shows you. (You may want to take with you something to record God's response or write it down on your return.)
- Option 2: Prayer lift. If you have a physically demanding task ahead, or if you can take what weighs you down to a gym or a workout, consider the power of contracting your core muscles. Activating your core is what grounds you; secures your foundation; and allows you to move, lift, or actively participate. As you work out, place your concern in the hands of a heavy-lifting God. (Be open to new insights, approaches, or ideas that occur as you go through your workout.)
- Option 3: Sleep on it. During sleep, the subconscious mind is a powerful place where God is very present. Offer a situation of concern to God as you retire for the night and see what the morning holds. (You may want to keep a notepad and pen by your bedside to write down what occurs to you immediately.) Whether it makes sense or not it, write down the words that come, because you won't remember them later. However, what you've written likely will make perfect sense in time.

Reflection

- What did you discover during or after walking/working out/sleeping? What surprised you?
- We tend to work our hardest to solve our hardest problems. When we leave our problems with God, God often shows us something new. It seems counterintuitive to give up rather than "ante up." How might working less on tough problems provide better solutions?
- Describe a time when you experienced the "peace that passes understanding," when you gave a situation to God and discovered a better way.
- Does God change God's mind? Does God change yours?

Prayer

O God, our human mind is not always sure what to believe. We want to believe the truth, but we're not sure how to find it. Our desire is to follow your truth, but it isn't always clear to us. Lead us to your truth. Lead us to your light. Illuminate us, we pray. Amen.

Thursday, Week 3

(Arm) Wrestling with God

Read Genesis 32.

> [The man] said, "Let me go, for the day is breaking." But Jacob said, "I will not let you go, unless you bless me."
>
> —Genesis 32:26

"I got winner!" shouts the next competitor, anxious to test his strength and skill against the reigning champion. When you're a fierce competitor, there's no stopping until you reach the top or topple trying. Not until you take on the toughest challenge and have proven yourself the champion will you feel sufficiently accomplished so that you may rest.

Combat wrestling always seems to me a brutal way to defeat an opponent, but arm wrestling seems somehow more civilized. Two competitors sit facing one another. They engage hand to hand as they jostle for position and grip, trying to get an edge. On the signal, they wrestle. Grunting and groaning, one pushes, the other gives; one thrusts, the other resists; one is nearly down and then recoils with a mighty force and, in one swift motion, thrusts the opponent's arm to the table.

What would it be like to wrestle with God, face-to-face and hand-to-hand? Would I be like Jacob, wrestling till daybreak? Would I demand a blessing from my opponent, who put my hip out of socket (a seriously low blow!) before I released him? Surely God, if God chose, could flatten me with one mighty blow. But God doesn't force. God doesn't overpower. God doesn't flatten. God resists, so we can gain strength.

I can imagine the sweat dripping from my temples, the angst showing in my red-faced effort, while God, sitting calmly, patiently, and serenely, waits for me to wear myself out or give myself up. How often do I engage in this wrestling match rather than acknowledging the superior strength, knowledge, and wisdom of Almighty God? Why do I persist in challenging when I know God's way is always a better way?

Activity

(See https://upperroombooks.com/madetomove.)

- Option 1: The Isometric workout. Find a sturdy wall. Steady your stance and then push as hard as you can against the wall. Did it move? Gather your strength and try again. Try it one more time with a moderate but prolonged effort. Can you sustain your effort for fifteen, thirty, sixty seconds? Any wall movement? How do you feel?
- Option 2: The Isometric press. Seated or standing, place your hands, palms together, in front of your face, elbows high. Press palms together as hard as you can and hold. Is one hand stronger? Resist! Is one hand weaker? Support it! Raise your hands slightly higher, to forehead level, and press again. Try again at belly button level. How did each press feel? Right vs. left? High, middle, low (forehead, face, belly button)? Which is easier? Harder? Consider why this might be.
- Option 3: The "isometric" suspension/"isotonic" triceps extension. Seated in a chair that has arm rests, press your forearms down into the arms of the chair and hold for fifteen, thirty, sixty seconds. Shift to place palms down on arms of the chair and push up, using only your arms. Can you lift yourself from the chair? Can you hold yourself there? Can you lift yourself all the way to standing? Can you repeat five times?

Reflection

- During this exercise, did your muscles fatigue? Did they give out and/or give up? When an effort is dangerously more than we can manage, our muscles are armed with a "shutdown" mechanism for safety called the Golgi tendon reflex. Why do you think God created us with a fail-safe release?
- When we push against a resistance that we are not strong enough to lift or move, our muscles are working by exerting effort, but we can't see any result. Does anything in your life right now feel like this (lots of exertion, but no movement)?
- Trainers design a strength workout to challenge muscles at submaximal strength, so that with repetition, muscles can get stronger and stronger. Which do you think works better: maximal exertion until failure or regular exertion to accomplish movement? Which one most resembles your approach to life? Do you use both approaches? Which works better?

Prayer:

Almighty and merciful God, though I am strong, I am but a mortal weakling in the face of some of life's challenges. Help me to know my own strength, supplying what I can and submitting where I must. Strengthen me in my trust of you and give me courage to walk in the sure knowledge of that strength. Amen.

Friday, Week 3

Blessed, Broken, Given Completely

Read Matthew 26:26-29.

> While they were eating, Jesus took a loaf of bread, and after blessing it he broke it, gave it to the disciples, and said, "Take, eat; this is my body."
>
> —Matthew 26:26

Susan's journey took her to a distant place, a different land, and a different people, yet she went with a full heart, ready to serve as a vacation Bible school teacher. The children came, excited to participate in all the activities and eager to make the craft Susan had planned. What joy it had been to gather the supplies for the children to make their own ceramic bowls. Surely, when they used them they would fondly remember their vacation Bible school experience and the love of their teacher. Susan smiled and waved as she watched the children depart, one by one. Then she stood stunned to see one child smash his bowl on the pavement outside.

What is our service worth if it is not appreciated? What if it is not received in love? I have often thought of Susan's recounting of this event and her brave response when asked how she felt: "A gift given is complete." It is not contingent on its acceptance, its utility, or its worth. Its whole value lies in its given-ness, already complete in the heart through which it was given. What happens next is not our responsibility.

The greatest gift ever given was a broken body and blood poured out at the table of grace that Christ has opened for all who would receive him. *This is my body, given for you. This is the blood of a new covenant, poured out for many, for the forgiveness of sins.* When we reach out to a friend, relative, or neighbor with a heart hoping to bless, it is not always received as a blessing. Sometimes there is shattering.

Humanity is full of brokenness, yet a hope-filled heart still reaches. But reaching leaves us exposed, sometimes to injury, counterpunch, or comeback. We take a risk when we extend a hand to someone we don't know or make an offer of friendship to someone who may mean us harm. Grasping the hand of another person in friendship, in promise, or in pledge, we can't be sure of the other person's intention. We only know ours. But our gift is complete if we have offered it with a sincere heart. At times, we are the ones who are broken and poured out.

Perhaps one day the child who returned from Bible school without his craft will remember Susan's act of generosity and know the love of God that was offered as a gift and that, in the breaking, the gift was given to him completely.

Activity

- On a piece of paper, copy the first verse of the book of Genesis: *In the beginning, God created the heavens and the earth.* Then, recopy it using your nondominant hand. Is one hand or one writing better? Why?
- Using your nondominant hand, copy the verse several more times. What did you observe about your hand? your writing?
- Read the verse as you've written it with your nondominant hand. Does this verse feel different to you in its new script?
- Throughout the day, challenge yourself to use your nondominant hand to perform your daily activities.

Reflection

- Do you prefer one side of your body? If yes, how does it feel to use your weaker side to perform simple tasks? Do you persevere? modify the task? compensate? adopt a different strategy?
- Humans tend to be "sided"; that is, we have a stronger side and a weaker side. What in your life do you choose to do strong-handed? Weak-handed? Both-handed? How do you hold what is most precious to you?
- Why do you suppose we are created with a "favored" side? Does God have a favorite side? Do you think creation is sided? Does it have stronger and weaker sides? Would God create this way? Why? Why not?

Prayer

Precious Jesus, you are God's loving hand extended to humanity, yet how often we fail to take hold, preferring our own way—only to watch our lives come crashing down. In your compassion, you extend both hands to pick us up and draw us into your holy embrace. Lead us to follow your example. May we give our all as you have given all, expecting nothing in return, in deepest gratitude for the forgiveness we have received in full. Amen.

Saturday, Week 3

Disobedience, Disorder, Out of Order

Read Matthew 7:24-27.

> "And the rain fell, and the floods came, and the winds blew and beat against that house, and it fell, and great was the fall of it."
>
> —Matthew 7:27 (ESV)

The fourth graders all rushed to line up for lunch, shuffling to assume their assigned places along the corridor. One pushed his way to the front, imploring the substitute teacher, "Does it really matter if we go out of order? We're all going to the same place." Pushing and shoving ensued. That fourth grader didn't see the need for order, so disruption was the result.

How often does our pushing or rushing to get ahead disorient and disorder us? The reality is, we count on order: order in the classroom; order in our household; order in our days, weeks, months, and years. We number things so we can put them in order. We list them so we can accomplish them in order. But what of the ordering of our lives as a whole?

While the world can seem very out of order at times, and, indeed, science tells us that the natural forces of entropy tend to move all things toward their disordered state, scripture makes clear that our God is a God of order. We know for certain that God cares about the arrangement of things: what's included, how much, and in what order it is added or applied. God knows how things go best, aware that leaving things out, putting things off, or getting by with a cheap substitute may disable the process or upend the project all together. God wants us to build on solid rock.

Our bodies, minds, and souls need structure in order to function. Our skeleton is a wonderful reminder of this, providing a solid framework from which we can push, pull, sit, stand, and move. Beginning as children we learn that order is best because order gives us a solid foundation from which to build. Then when entropy scatters and disruption comes, we will not be washed away.

Health Wheel

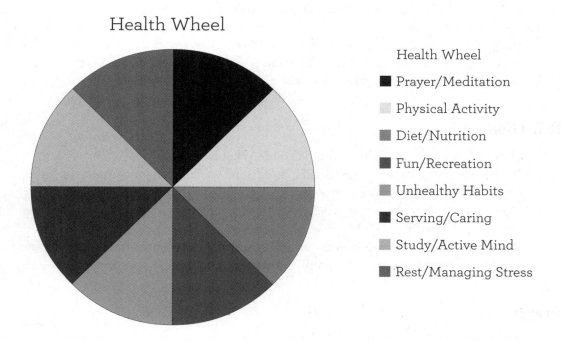

Health Wheel
- ■ Prayer/Meditation
- □ Physical Activity
- ■ Diet/Nutrition
- ■ Fun/Recreation
- ■ Unhealthy Habits
- ■ Serving/Caring
- ■ Study/Active Mind
- ■ Rest/Managing Stress

Activity

Good physical health demands a balance among the components of physical fitness: endurance, strength, flexibility, and body composition. Let's expand on this idea to consider the components of whole life fitness, or wholeness, which encompasses health in body, mind, and spirit.

- On the sample health wheel (see page 55), I have taken the components of a healthy lifestyle (physical/bodily, mental, emotional/psychological, and spiritual), and separated them into the supporting lifestyle practices listed to the right of the wheel. I have also included an "unhealthy habits" segment so we can consider lifestyle habits or patterns of behavior that need to be reduced or removed as we seek a healthy lifestyle.
- How balanced are you in your pursuit of a healthy body, mind, and spirit? Draw your own personal health wheel; include all the components shown. Score yourself from 0 to 10 in each category. (0 = I spend no time on this; 10 = I spend all my time on this.) If 0 is the center of your wheel and 10 is on the outer circumference, place a dot along each line indicating your score, from 0 to 10.
- Draw a new circle by connecting the dots on your wheel. (Disregard the dot in "unhealthy habits" for this part of the exercise.) How smooth is your circle? How balanced is your lifestyle? How well would your health wheel roll?
- What habits or patterns of behavior are giving you a flat tire?

Reflection

- How ordered is your health? What is solid? What is sand?
- Which category deserves particular attention? Which category gets too much attention? Would you add a category? _____
- How might you achieve better balance by ordering or paying more detailed attention to your health?
- What benefits might a more balanced and healthier lifestyle provide? What changes would you need to make to accomplish this?

Prayer

Creator God, you made the earth and everything in it according to your perfect plan. What is it like when we preempt that plan with our own—when we run ahead of your plan to accomplish our desires or when we push ahead? Abide with us, we pray. Infuse us with your patience and embolden us to address what is out of order in our lives to set it in its rightful place. Help us offer our whole selves and our whole lives to you, gladly. Amen.

4

Body Bent

Because of the LORD's great love we are not consumed,
    for his compassions never fail.
They are new every morning;
    great is your faithfulness.
I say to myself, "The LORD is my portion;
    therefore I will wait for him."

—Lamentations 3:22-24 (NIV)

The burdens of this world can weigh us down. This week let us consider how bending in humility is the place we can best ask for God's help to strengthen and guide us.

Sunday, Week 4

Nourishment for the Journey

Read 1 Kings 19:1-9.

> The angel of the LORD came a second time, touched him, and said, "Get up and eat, otherwise the journey will be too much for you."
>
> —1 Kings 19:7

Have you ever come to Sunday feeling like Elijah? Have you been exhausted from a week of work and worries, emotionally drained by colleagues or perhaps family—served out, stressed out, and spent? When all you want is a bed and a good long sleep, any broom bush will do. If we barely manage to muster the energy to worship, the self we bring is far from whole. We gratefully collapse onto the mercy of God. "Lord, what a week it has been," we tell God, and dredge up the mind, body, and soul that we have poured out all week, asking God to help us recover. Again.

God does come to us knowing our exhaustion, but instead of pity, the Lord offers bread and water. Life can be demanding and sometimes devastating, but more than rescue, God wants to revive us with what we'll need for the coming days. God doesn't want us trapped in a continuous cycle of exhaust, collapse, repair, and repeat. God provides what we need to move along, even if, for the moment, that provision is only enough to help us take the next step.

Surely, there are times when hardship and trial are so monumental that we can only fall into the arms of Jesus and allow him to carry us. But most of life is lived in the rolling hills. If after each exertion we allow time to adapt and recover, we'll find ourselves a bit stronger, more resilient, more capable, and more adept. This is the process that propels us toward the mountain before our Lord, where we listen, not with trepidation or foreboding, but with expectation and anticipation to the question addressed to us: "What are you doing here, _____?"

Sunday's respite opens us to our Lord who sends us forth with provision and purpose.

Activity

- How much sleep do you get on an average night? 5 How many consistent number of hours? Do you wake and retire at approximately the same time? Yes
- As you retire each night this week, envision yourself standing before the mountain of God with a cloak over your face, listening for the gentle whisper of God. Don't worry if you fall asleep listening.
- Use a notepad and pen or pencil next to your bed to record how you slept each night. Is your sleep restful, restless, fitful, or deep? Do you awaken frequently? Do you return to sleep easily? If you awaken, is it helpful to listen for the gentle whisper?
- Did you dream? If you can recall your dream, record it. Did you wake up with some insight? Record the insight as well.

Reflection

- Did the practice of attending to your sleep and sleep patterns change how you slept? On good-sleep days, what seemed to help? On poor-sleep days, what seemed disruptive?
- Did you record any dreams or insights? Did they surprise you? What did you learn?
- Why do you think God created us with a need for sleep?
- Psalm 121:4 tells us, "He who watches over Israel will neither slumber nor sleep" (NIV). What comfort do you feel from this promise?

Prayer:

Lord, thank you for not giving up on me, even when I feel like giving up on myself. Your bread and water sustain me in a way that nothing else in the world does. You, Jesus, broken bread and poured out wine, are food and drink for a famished and parched humanity. Let us eat and drink and find rest and renewal in your love and care along our way. Amen.

Monday, Week 4

Heart Yielded or Road Closed?

Read 1 Corinthians 9:24-27.

> Do you not know that in a race the runners all compete, but only one receives the prize? Run in such a way that you may win it.
>
> —1 Corinthians 9:24

Which sign do you prefer? *Road Closed* or *Yield*? *Road Closed* means go no further, you've reached the end, turn around. Despite the disappointment and possible consequences of having to turn around, I like the sign because the message is clear. *Yield*, on the other hand, is uncomfortable because it's ambiguous. I have to decide if and when it's safe to proceed.

Occasionally, on a low-traffic day, deciding when to go is easy. But when there is traffic; if I'm in a hurry; on a deadline; or if there's a limited quantity available on a first-come, first-served basis, then the yield sign is tempting to ignore. Because if I stop and look, I might have to yield, and that will cost me time, position, and perhaps my place on the winner's podium.

But pace comes at a price; it's tough to take sharp turns at that speed, not to mention the dangers of missing the *Road Closed* sign until it's too late. A heart yielded to God in our life's race need not worry about missing the signs or about those who fail to yield or who push their way ahead. No, a heart yielded to God seeks to run the race on pace to finish it. Our ultimate objective is not to beat all others but to run in such a way that we may win, and this motivates us to sustain our effort and speed while keeping our eyes on the prize.

We all have a finish line; some of us may come to it sooner than expected. It is better that we learn to pace ourselves so that we may run in such a way that when we cross it, we have run like winners.

Activity

Choose something from your heart-healthy grab bag. Sometimes in our excitement we may start off too fast and sabotage our pacing. During today's activity, try these two simple methods to gauge your effort and maintain your intended pace.

- Option 1: The Rate of Perceived Exertion (RPE) scale measures how hard exercise feels. The scale goes from 0-10, with 0 = "no effort at all" and 10 = "very, very hard effort." (It is also a scientifically validated means to estimate the intensity of workload as a percentage of your maximum effort, i.e., a score of 7 = ~70 percent effort) Monitor your effort before beginning, midway, and at the end of your heart-healthy activity today and record your "scores" according to the RPE scale.

Rating	Description
0	NO EFFORT AT ALL
0.5	VERY, VERY LIGHT
1	VERY LIGHT
2	FAIRLY LIGHT
3	MODERATE
4	SOMEWHAT HARD
5	
6	VERY HARD
7	
8	
9	
10	VERY VERY HARD (MAXIMAL)

- Option 2: The Talk Test requires a companion (or imagined companion) with whom you attempt to speak out loud during exertion. Maintaining a pace at which you can comfortably converse prevents overexertion. If talking becomes labored or impossible, reduce your effort to maintain a constant pace. Exercising partners can offer this feedback to each other.

Reflection

- How did your effort feel today? What was your score? Did early exertion feel harder or easier than when you got going? What felt hardest? Easiest? Was it helpful to give it a number? As you become accustomed to regular activity, what used to be hard may feel easier. What change have you noticed over our four weeks of heart-healthy activity?
- How did conversing during the activity help you monitor how hard you were working? What effect did your partner have on your perception of effort?
- There are times in life when you feel so out of breath it becomes difficult to talk to God. How might it help to apply the RPE or the Talk Test to these times? What person of the triune God (Father, Son, or Holy Spirit) would you talk to? What might you talk about?

Prayer

O Lord, as hard as I try to keep a steady pace, I often find myself cruising with the traffic and picking up speed. Your signs are all along my way, and I don't want to miss a single one. Grow in me a willingness to yield to others rather than a desire to race ahead. Help me run my own race as you would have me run it, putting one foot ahead of the other all the way to the finish line. Amen.

Tuesday, Week 4

God, the Good Listener

Read Philippians 4:6-9.

Do not worry about anything, but in everything by prayer and supplication with thanksgiving let your requests be made known to God. And the peace of God, which surpasses all understanding, will guard your hearts and your minds in Christ Jesus.

—Philippians 4:6-7

A wise and faith-filled friend once asked me, "I wonder what our collective prayers sound like to God." I imagined a tremendous gathering of the faithful—all ages, nations, races, colors, and languages—petitioning and praising, repenting and confessing, the voiced and voiceless, whose prayers were offered plaintively by the Spirit as wordless groans. (See Romans 8:26-27.) The din would be deafening for anyone but God. What majesty and power there is in that cacophony, but I can't help wondering how in the midst of it all that God can possibly hear me.

In those times, I take such comfort in the invitation Jesus gave to the children: "Let the little children come to me, and do not stop them; for it is to such as these that the kingdom of heaven belongs" (Matt. 19:14). Now children being children—rambunctious, excited, spirited, and playful—once Jesus invites them, do you suppose they come solemnly, waiting their turn, one by one, and in a neat line? No, I imagine they all rush to Jesus, begging to be the one who got to sit on his lap. And Jesus, being Jesus, doesn't turn anyone away. He listens to each little voice. Even the ones who are shy, I imagine he listens them into speaking.

We, children of God, have access to our own audience with the Master, thanks to Jesus the Christ. God welcomes each voice lifted, whether resounding in the din or moaning in silence, together in holy chorus, or whispered one by one. With our voices as instruments of praise and prayer, we may freely appeal to our listening God. Even if our song is halting and unsure like a child's, we are assured that God listens in love to each one of us, for it is to such as these that the kingdom of heaven belongs.

Activity

- Today, challenge yourself to listen, even when you have the urge to speak. Listen actively to others by showing your interest visually, verbally, and bodily. Nod and encourage with your demeanor and your words. Listen the other into speaking.
- If you are in or near a noisy place, take a moment to listen to all that's around you and consider what this sounds like to God. If there are many simultaneous conversations, can you home in on one voice? Is there a voice you recognize? How are you able to distinguish it from the others? Did anyone use your name or call to you? Did that voice or sound rise above the others?

- If you are able, go to a public place to listen and observe without speaking. What do you notice about the way people interact with each other in conversation?

Reflection

- How did your active listening impact the person(s) you listened to today? What effect did your listening have on the noisy public place? Which was more comfortable for you? Why?
- God hears our prayers in quiet, private places and in loud, public places. When does quiet seem loud and loud seem quiet? Why do we seek silence with God? Why are we often uncomfortable in silence with another person? with God?
- If you felt sure God was listening to you in prayer, how would that affect the way you pray? How does it affect what you say? How do you listen to God in prayer?

Prayer

Parent God, thank you for taking time to listen to us, even though you know our thoughts before we think them and our words before we speak them. You created us with ears to hear and voices to speak so that through the Spirit, we may speak and listen to you. Following your example, may we learn when to speak and when to listen to one another. Amen.

Wednesday, Week 4

Shifting Focus to See Clearly

Read Proverbs 3:1-12.

> Do not be wise in your own eyes;
>   fear the LORD and shun evil.

This will bring health to your body
  and nourishment to your bones.

—Proverbs 3:7-8 (NIV)

"Just because they said it, doesn't make it true," a kind friend once assured me when I had endured particularly unkind words flung my way. Sometimes we need a reminder not to believe everything we hear. Deception may promote itself as truth, even in our own minds. To distinguish falsity from truth, we need to test what we see and hear so we can discern what is good. To reject any kind of evil, we must recognize it, call it out, and dismiss it.

It would be so much more convenient if life came with a truth guarantee. But God did not create us with minds set to coast on autopilot. Rather than be passive participants, we're meant to actively engage with our world, plotting a course by careful attention and continuous course correction. Opposition teaches us focus.

A team of nine-year-old soccer players I once coached showed this to me. They diligently practiced the footskills I taught them, working hard to get their form just right, but their moves were still slow and ineffective. To hone their skills, they needed the pressure of a defender—someone trying to steal the ball. Against opposition, they disciplined themselves, learning to perform with speed and accuracy. Their newfound confidence allowed them to beat their opponent with sharply executed skills.

Perhaps God has placed opposition in our paths for exactly this reason: to teach us to shun evil and focus on what's good, honorable, excellent, and true. By cultivating this, what opposes us will not defeat us.

Activity

- With both eyes open, spot a nearby, narrow object, like a tree, fence post, etc. Line up the finger of one hand with this object. Do this quickly and automatically, without thinking too much. Do you see two fingers, one more clearly than the other? Close your right eye. What happens? Does your finger appear to move? Close your left eye. Is the result the same? Different? (This is your brain using "binocular" vision to compare input from both eyes and achieve a 3D image. It is also a simple test of brain side dominance.)
- Repeat the above, lining up your finger at arm's length with an object in the far distance. First, focus your vision on your finger. Can you see it clearly? Now, shift

your focus to look at the object in the distance. Can you see it clearly? (Your brain is able to accommodate to see both distant and near vision.)

- Though 3D vision and accommodation vary among people and may change as we age, our brains are magnificently designed intentionally to shift perspective. Try these activities throughout your day. If persons ask you what you're doing, invite them to try it. What is their reaction?

Reflection

- Did you know your eyes have two different ways of "seeing"? They adjust near and far and compare right and left. Why do you think our brains have this capacity? How would life look without 3D? Without the contrast of dimension?
- The ability to accommodate our vision—to toggle between near and distance vision—assists humans with perception, but this may be impaired if we don't have perfect eyesight, and this may decline somewhat as our eyes age. Some rely on corrective lenses to improve eyesight. Is there a lens which helps us with 3D truth acuity? Could Christ be considered such a lens?
- What would happen if we inverted that lens and turned it inward? What might our new vision show us? How might the lens of Christ assist our vision? our perception? Can our capacity for visual accommodation help?
- Fold a large piece of poster paper in half. On one side, sketch what you see through outward 3D lenses. On the other side, sketch what you see through inward 3D lenses. Overlay the lens of Christ. How do the images change? Color over them in bright colors.

Prayer

Lord, you provide light so that we may see clearly, even when clouds and darkness threaten to make us stumble. Help us stay focused on you, even as you perfect our vision. Help us trust that even what you have allowed to oppose us is meant for your good purposes. Cultivate in us a discerning spirit that seeks to see only you and what you see. Amen.

Thursday, Week 4

Casting Off the Burden of Perfect

Read Luke 10:38-42.

> The Lord answered her, "Martha, Martha, you are worried and distracted by many things; there is need of only one thing. Mary has chosen the better part, which will not be taken away from her."
>
> —Luke 10:41-42

Company is coming, and you want the guest room to be perfect. To impress the professor your paper needs to be perfect. For that promotion, this proposal had better be perfect. If we're not careful, perfectionism can become a way of life, leaving us unable ever to settle for less than exactly right. This can create a burden that we can't bear. While excellence is a commendable objective, perfection is God's job.

How familiar the story of Martha's scurrying to serve her special guest, Jesus, while sister Mary sits at the Lord's feet. "Martha, Martha, you are worried and distracted by many things; there is need of only one thing" (Luke 10:41). The Lord can see that Martha, bent under the weight of her own intentions, needs to unload her burden. His message: *Your intentions are admirable, but your soul is heavy. Let me help you choose the good portion; come and rest.*

God invites us to lay down what is heaviest—the fear that we won't be acceptable, won't make the grade, or won't measure up. Fear fuels our anxious attempts at self-perfecting. In love, Jesus tells us to surrender that—not to make us feel like weaklings but like "meeklings." Meekness, he can use. No longer bent under that troubling weight, we can do the heavy lifting of life, strong and upright. Perhaps then when we look in the mirror, we'll allow ourselves to see as God sees us and love ourselves with that love—the perfect love that casts out all fear. (See 1 John 4:18.)

Activity

- Option 1: Weight lifting. If you regularly train with weights, how is your form? Use a mirror to check the position of your torso and lower back when you lift. (If available, ask a trainer or experienced lifter to help.) Locking the lumbar spine in a strong position (not rounded or collapsed) forms the strong base for weight lifting (using dumbbells, barbells, free weights, or Olympic lifts).
- Option 2: Lifestyle "lifting." Stand and tighten your abdominal muscles, becoming aware of your lumbar (lower back) curve and posture. Our spine is our fulcrum for all movement. Standing, bending, kneeling, and twisting all require firm support from our strong core. Kneeling at the Communion rail or bending to tie our shoes can be reminders to us: "contract your core" to distribute the weight of bending and to support you when you stand.

Reflection

- How heavy is the life-burden you are lifting? Are you waiting until it is unbearable before you ask for help?
- Do you feel responsible for some weight you are bearing alone? Have you asked God for help?
- Is there something heavy that is challenging you to lift it? What core support do you need to put in place to lift it safely?
- What, in your life, would provide needed respite if you were to distribute the weight?

Prayer

Lord Jesus, I confess that _____ puts me out of balance. No matter how hard I try, I can't right myself. I need your counter-balance to tip me back upright. Thank you for bearing the weight of this with me and for leading me to a level place. Amen.

Friday, Week 4

I Want to Be That Kind of Friend

Read Mark 2:1-12.

> Some men came, bringing to him a paralyzed man, carried by four of them.
>
> —Mark 2:3 (NIV)

Bent nearly double under hurricane force winds, the palm tree's branches thrashed as driving rains whipped its fronds mercilessly and sent debris hurtling past. Any minute, the tree could uproot and be swept skyward. Yet, after the eye of the storm passed and winds abated, the palm still stood upright, apparently unharmed. Palm trees are strong, but the key to their resilience is flexibility. They can bend without breaking.

While standing firm is essential for foundations, rigidity is rarely an admirable human trait. More often the challenges and storms of life demand resilience, a healthy mix of strength and flexibility. Perhaps that's why the story of the four men carrying their paralyzed friend to Jesus so delights me. The man's immobility moves his friends to act. Seeing that they can't get in via the door, they haul him onto the roof and dig through to let him down at the very feet of Jesus! Now that's strength and flexibility!

What kind of friendship inspires that kind of devotion? And what kind of faith moves it? The man must have been gold to his friends—trusted, reliable, compassionate, and caring—a guy who was there when his friends needed him. Then, when the man needed Jesus, the friends were not to be denied!

I want to be that kind of friend. If someone dear to me can't find the courage or is paralyzed by fear to do the one thing that would heal him or her, I want a faith strong enough to bring a friend to Jesus and flexible enough to lay him or her down at Jesus' feet. What a moment it would be to watch from the roof as my friend picked up his mat and walked home on his own two feet.

Activity

(See https://upperroombooks.com/madetomove.)

- Sit upright in a sturdy chair with your feet resting firmly on the floor and at least shoulder width apart. Extend your arms straight out to either side. Contract the muscles of your torso to keep firm posture, bend/lean to one side, attempting to touch the floor with your fingertips on that side. Try not to bend forward at the waist. (Arms stay in a "T" throughout the movement, so at the point of touch, fingers of the other hand stretch up toward the ceiling.)
- Return to sitting upright. Firm your posture. Now bend/lean and touch your fingertips to the other side. Resist collapsing forward at the waist when you lean to the side. Go slowly as you near the floor to lower your fingers down to touch. See how many side-to-side touches you can do while keeping good form.

Reflection

- This activity requires both strength and flexibility. Is bending to one side easier than to the other? Were you able to touch the floor on both sides? Which side is stronger? Which feels more flexible? (Fun fact: when you bend to the right, it is your left side that is supplying the strength against gravity and vice versa. Can you tell this?)
- Strength and flexibility work together at our joints to provide healthy movement, but a blow from the side can sometimes throw us off balance if we're not expecting it. Have you ever been bent or knocked off balance by something you didn't see coming? Did it uproot you? Make you more resilient? How?
- Are there people in your life who are strong but not very flexible? Flexible but not very strong? How has faith made you stronger? more flexible? more resilient? What additional work does faith have to do in you?

Prayer

Dear Jesus, many people in my world suffer ailments and endure hardships that you alone can heal, but they haven't met you or are afraid to get to know you. Build in me a faith that has the courage to carry them to wherever you are and the flexibility to find just the right way to set them before you. Amen.

Saturday, Week 4

Putting Discipline to Work

Read Hebrews 12:7-13.

> Now, discipline always seems painful rather than pleasant at the time, but later it yields the peaceful fruit of righteousness to those who have been trained by it.
>
> —Hebrews 12:11

"The vision of a champion is someone who is bent over, drenched in sweat, at the point of exhaustion when no one else is watching," writes renowned women's soccer coach Anson Dorrance in praise of his rising soccer star Mia Hamm.* It's one thing to *know* what to do; it's quite another thing to *do* it. When one takes the initiative, even when no one is watching; that's the stuff of champions.

God wants to make each of us a champion in life. The One who created us knows what we're made of and has given us our instructions, but it's up to us to put them into practice. That takes discipline; there's no short cut. In deciding to follow Christ, we make the choice to endure potential hardship for the sake of being disciplined as a son or daughter of our loving God.

God doesn't just deliver inspirational lectures and hand out final exams. God loves us too much for that and knows only too well that when we are faced with a life-sized assignment, our first response will likely be, "Do you have something a bit less demanding? Something seasonal, perhaps with a shorter-term commitment?" Wherever possible, we tend to prefer the superficial skim rather than the deep dive, the makeover to the deep cleansing.

---

*Anson Dorrance and Gloria Averbuch, *The Vision of a Champion: Advice and Inspiration from the World's Most Successful Women's Soccer Coach* (Ann Arbor, MI: Huron River Press, 2002), 1.

God knows that for transformation to happen, we must dig deep. To bring order and direction to our lives and to invest them fully with the power of the Holy Spirit, we must be disciplined. Not punished, as discipline is commonly understood, but held to the highest standard, voluntarily. That is, we must dedicate ourselves to the practice of spiritual disciplines such as prayer and worship, confession and fasting, and sacrificial service and giving, in order to align ourselves with God's will. These spiritual discipline "assignments" shape our nature and conform our character.

I can just imagine our Almighty Coach watching from a distance as we, bent over and drenched in sweat, are spent nearly to the point of exhaustion. Coach knows the harvest of righteousness and peace being produced in those being trained by it. If we think no one is watching, we're wrong.

Activity

- Look back at your Health Wheel from last Saturday. Review the healthy lifestyle categories and any that you may have added. Which practices contribute most to physical health? Which contribute most to mental health? Emotional health? Spiritual health? Which span more than one category? (You may find that penciling these into your wheel (B M E S) helps affirm your efforts.)
- Considering the wheel categories, how have you spent your time this week? Give yourself a score (0–10) in each category. How have your scores changed since last week? Is your connect-the-dot circle smoother? What unhealthy habit have you admitted and begun to address?
- What areas feel fuller? Do you feel more filled in some areas? more depleted? Since your time and energy are fixed quantities, what time and energy did you spend differently this week? What shifts did you see?

Reflection

- Are you a naturally disciplined person, a natural rule follower? In some areas but not others? What do you find easy to be disciplined about? What presents a challenge?
- Have you made changes in your lifestyle behaviors? Do some things resist change? Does giving yourself a "score" feel motivating? indicting? What have your efforts toward better balance shown you about yourself?

- Not only our spiritual health but also our physical, mental, and emotional health matter to God. If God's discipline is training you, what do you need to do to become God's champion?

Prayer

Parent God, I like discipline. I just do not like to be disciplined. Please help me to accept the correction you have for me, knowing that it will do me good and better equip me to do your work. Help me stay committed over the long term, even when life gets really hard. I want to be your champion, now and forever. Amen.

5

Body Rebuilt

Consequently, you are no longer foreigners and strangers, but fellow citizens with God's people and also members of his household, built on the foundation of the apostles and prophets, with Christ Jesus himself as the chief cornerstone. In him the whole building is joined together and rises to become a holy temple in the Lord. And in him you too are being built together to become a dwelling in which God lives by his Spirit.

—Ephesians 2:19-22 (NIV)

Our bodies and our lives are constantly under construction. As Christians we have Christ as our chief cornerstone. This week, let us commit ourselves fully to God's renovation, already underway.

Sunday, Week 5

The Rhythm of Rest

Read Hebrews 4:1-13.

> A sabbath rest still remains for the people of God; for those who enter God's rest also cease from their labors as God did from his. Let us therefore make every effort to enter that rest, so that no one may fall through such disobedience as theirs.
>
> —Hebrews 4:9

"I don't want to rest. That makes me feel really sad," a young mother told me. With two young children, a new husband, and an exciting full-time job, resting felt like giving up or giving in. There was work to be done and she wanted to be doing it. To her, resting felt like resignation.

But life must cycle between work and rest. After a time of building we need a time to recover. And the process of rebuilding, which goes on in us throughout our lives, requires both breaking down and building up. Ironically, it's work that breaks us down and rest that builds us back up. Without rest, there is just breakdown.

Work and rest are not opposites but aggregates, each necessary for the full expression of the other. While working to "get life right" is essential to the Christian life, resting from our work is God-commanded for a reason. The world often urges us to hurry along, yet we need only look to the example of our God who spent the seventh day resting from the work done in creation, not because God needed to take a breather but because God knew we would.

In each of us, God has crafted a blueprint for our completion and provided the raw materials for its accomplishment. We are continuously being built and rebuilt according to God's timing and specifications. Filled with the Holy Spirit, our bodies host the meeting of our heart, soul, mind, and strength as our construction proceeds. In the rhythm of work and rest, hearts squeeze and release, lungs inspire and expire, minds figure and fidget, muscles contract and relax. While all systems are go, they are not always going full blast. There is a rhythm to all of life. Rest is what allows us to keep the beat.

Activity

- Today, be early to every activity on your calendar and allow extra time transitioning to the next thing. (Warning: You may need to reschedule some things or rearrange your schedule to accomplish this.) Allow things to take their time.
- What did you do with your "extra" time?
- How did it feel? To whom did you give it? What did it give to you?
- How can you allow for extra time this week?

Reflection

- Not all rest is the same. Passive (do nothing) rest is better for healing. Active (gentle movement) rest is better for recovery from effort, gradually returning the body to a state of readiness. Did allowing extra time feel active or passive to you?
- Was allowing extra time easy or difficult? Did the experience surprise you? How?
- What is God showing you about rest? About time? About this time in your life?
- What do you think God did while God was resting?

Prayer

God of the seventh day, slow me when my desire to accomplish and build has me rushing from one thing to the next. Remind me that your natural rhythm of rest and renewal is essential to keeping all things in working order. The me you are making will be accomplished in your good time. Thank you for your patience while I am under construction. Amen.

Monday, Week 5

What Are the Vital Signs in a Christian Life?

Read 2 Corinthians 4:16-18.

> Therefore we do not lose heart. Though outwardly we are wasting away, yet inwardly we are being renewed day by day.
>
> —2 Corinthians 4:16 (NIV)

Few people are more motivated to get heart-healthy than those who have suffered a heart attack.

I know because they greeted me at 6:45 a.m. daily, when I arrived to unlock the doors of the facility where we held the cardiac rehab program. Their doctors had put the fear of God in them to start exercising, and they complied religiously. During exercise sessions, we monitored their vital signs like blood pressure, pulse, respiration, and EKG, to make sure their hearts were working properly. If there was a concern, we knew it right away. This gave them the confidence they needed to work their way back to full fitness. They knew they were safe with us.

When life takes a toll on our hearts, it's good to know we have a safe place to do the work of healing. It's not easy to recover our stamina after illness or injury, but we don't lose heart. Because though "outwardly we are wasting away, yet inwardly we are being renewed day by day." (See 2 Corinthians. 4:16.) The heart God is restoring in you and in me won't be ailing like our old one; it will be good as new. God doesn't just resuscitate, shocking us back to our old life; God resurrects us into new life.

That is a great motivation to get moving! Our rehabbed hearts will take us to the places we're most needed, and where there is vital work to be done. It's okay to let competitors sprint ahead if they want to push the pace. *Run your heart out,* God seems to say. *You're safe with me.*

Activity

- What can you do now that you couldn't do when we first began the *Made to Move* journey together? (Can you go farther? faster? harder? for longer? Can you cover more challenging terrains?) Consistency builds progress. What progress do you see?
- Interval training (alternating times of higher and lower intensity activity) is a safe way to progress your fitness. In performing your heart grab bag activity of choice today, alternate brief periods of slightly increased intensity into your effort (i.e., five-minute walk, one-minute jog, repeated to end of session).
- Recreational option: Use a visual cue (after every three mailboxes) or auditory cue (after every two songs on headphones) to switch from higher to lower intensity. Were you able to sustain the higher effort? What helped?
- At the end of the session, be sure to cool down with slower movement to allow blood to be circulated back to your heart and to prevent its pooling in your legs. (We discussed yesterday the benefits of active rest for recovery.)
- If you'd like to set a goal for your cardio training, see http://fit2finish.com/5k-run-training-plan-this-schedule-will-get-you-across-the-finish-line/. There are many online resources available, depending on your experience and goals.
- HIIT (High Intensity Interval Training) has recently become popular. Caution: High intensity workouts without someone to monitor your form can result in injury. (See https://en.wikipedia.org/wiki/High-intensity_interval_training.)

Reflection

- How are you making progress toward becoming healthier or more fit? Do you monitor your vital signs (heart rate, blood pressure, exertional breathing)? Are they showing improvement?
- What are the vital signs of a Christian life? Are they showing improvement in you?
- What was wasting away in you that is now being renewed?

Prayer

Lord God, more than anything, I want to live a vital life, but sometimes the weakness of my heart holds me back. Help me believe that the heart you began beating in me is being renewed in your love, day by day. Grant me patience with myself when I falter or have to slow down, so I might encourage others whose hearts are on the mend too. Amen.

Tuesday, Week 5

Hungering for the Bread of Life

Read John 6:32-35.

> Then Jesus said to them, "Very truly, I tell you, it was not Moses who gave you the bread from heaven, but it is my Father who gives you the true bread from heaven. For the bread of God is that which comes down from heaven and gives life to the world." They said to him, "Sir, give us this bread always."
>
> Jesus said to them, "I am the bread of life. Whoever comes to me will never be hungry, and whoever believes in me will never be thirsty."
>
> —John 6:35

I recall the blessed aroma that wafted from my grandmother's kitchen as a loaf of bread baked to a golden brown. Over years of watching and helping like an acolyte at her elbow, I learned the secrets of bread-making: the mixing, the shaping, the rhythmic kneading, until the texture was smooth as silk. Cover the dough and wait. What a delight to see that it had doubled in size! Punch it down and let it rise again. Oh, the luscious aroma that preceded our buttery feast was the product of hours of loving effort, and all very much worth the wait. But unlike cookie dough, there was no tasting before its time.

There is nothing like freshly baked bread to bring fellowship around a table, and no one like Jesus to bring the bread of life. "Whoever comes to me will never be hungry, and whoever believes in me will never be thirsty" (John 6:35). As the tasty loaf we consume nourishes us, it becomes part of our very constitution. Whatever we feed our bodies becomes a living part of us, the bread of Communion included. The stuff of our Lord becomes the stuff of us.

As we offer the blessing before our meal, we acknowledge God's presence with us and provision for us at the table set before us. "Come, Lord Jesus, be our guest, and let these gifts to us be blessed. Amen." That was my family's grace. As I grew in age and faith I added, "and for the hands which have prepared it, we give thanks." Those hands, kneading, shaping, and bidding us rise, are lovingly supplied by Christ, so that all who are gathered at the table may never go hungry. Thanks be to God, who sent Christ and prepares for us. What feasting there will be! It'll be worth the wait.

Activity

- Option 1: Fast from one meal today.
- Option 2: Fast from processed food today. Eat only fresh food. Food that looks like what it is, not packaged or modified: chicken, not chicken nuggets; fish, not fish sticks.
- Option 3: Fast from fast food today. Prepare what you eat with your own hands.
- Before every meal today, come to the table of grace and give thanks.

Reflection

- If you grew up saying grace before meals, why do you think your family observed the practice? Do you say grace now? Why or why not?
- Waiting for our food makes us hungry. How does hunger feel? What does hunger do?
- Describe what it would be like to be truly hungry. In addition to feeling hungry, what other feelings might you have? Are people hungry for both food and for God in your community? How might you feed them with both?

Prayer

Jesus, bread of life, you have filled me with good things. Yet too often I forget that you are the source of all of them. Use my fasting, my time of dedication, and my small sacrifice to show me those near me who are hungering for what I have to give. Incline my heart and soul toward them that I may freely and gladly give as you have given so generously to me. Amen.

Wednesday, Week 5

Clearing a Way Through Our Fog

Read 1 Corinthians 13:8-13.

> For now we see in a mirror, dimly, but then we will see face to face. Now I know only in part; then I will know fully, even as I have been fully known.
>
> —1 Corinthians 13:12

Have you ever tried to navigate through fog so thick you could hardly see your hand in front of your face? Yet to get where you're going, you have to keep moving. If you can just keep the taillights of the car in front of you in view, you'll make steady progress toward your destination. Wouldn't it be nice, though, if we could clear the view all the way to our destination with a deep inhale and a hearty blow along the horizon?

Alas, life doesn't present itself that way. On a good day, equipped with my tiny hand-held blow dryer, I can barely clear a space large enough to see myself in the foggy bathroom mirror. That, God assures, is all we need to proceed. Each one of us is handcrafted with a mind designed to see uniquely through our own clearing. This is why our wise and benevolent Creator has placed us in the company of others who see differently: so we can lend perspective to one another.

We know that for now we see as in a mirror, only dimly, and know only in part, but one day we shall see face to face and know fully, even as we are fully known. Between now and then, we need not navigate blindly. For Christ, the Word of God, becomes flesh in us if we ask the Spirit of God to help us see. And one day, in the gathering of the faithful, the fog will be lifted and perfection revealed, and all of us will see it together.

Activity

- Practice the presence of God using one of the techniques or activities we have already learned: the breath prayer, Lord's Prayer, sound of sheer silence, sit on Jesus' knee, or let the Spirit intercede in words you can't find. Sit in the stillness of this prayer.
- Bring yourself to Jesus. Thank him, face-to-face, not just for what he's done but also for who he is. Give thanks for the suffering he endured and the hope he represents.
- Whatever you need to discuss, God will listen. Read Psalms 32, 51, and 139. Choose one psalm with words that express what you want to say to God through Jesus the Christ. Offer what you say aloud in prayer. Then, listen for what Jesus says to you.
- If you wish to take this further, explore this dialogue in writing. Fold a sheet of paper lengthwise, creating two vertical columns. At the top of the left column, write "Me." Label the right column "Jesus." (The left-hand column is for your words. The right-hand column is for Jesus' response to you.) Imagine that you are sitting alone with Jesus. Say in writing what is on your heart. Listen and write the responses you hear.

Reflection

- How did you experience this face-to-face encounter with Christ?
- What was surprising about what you said to Jesus? What was surprising about what Jesus said to you?
- Do you have the hope of forgiveness? What will you do with this hope?

Prayer

Jesus, my Lord and Savior, I confess that some days I see clearly what you ask of me, but other days your will seems foggy. Send your Spirit to lead me through the fog and redirect me from anything that would send me off course. Clear my way to you. Amen.

Thursday, Week 5

Flexing Our Spiritual Muscles and Donning Our Spiritual Super Suit

Read 1 Samuel 17 and Ephesians 6:10-18.

> For our struggle is not against flesh and blood, but against the rulers, against the authorities, against the powers of this dark world and against the spiritual forces of evil in the heavenly realms.
>
> —Ephesians 6:2 (NIV)

Imagine how young David must have looked trying on King Saul's armor. Bent under the weight of the trappings of war to which he was unaccustomed, David shucked it all in favor of a slingshot and five smooth stones. Ironically, he found the garb of war unwieldy and awkward, yet facing a nine-foot-tall Philistine did not weigh heavily on him. That boy had some God-confidence!

God's mighty power is available to all who hope in the Lord, but as Paul warns us in his letter to the Ephesians, our struggle is not merely against flesh and blood but "against the rulers, against the authorities, against the powers of this dark world" (Eph. 6:12, NIV). For that engagement, we're going to need God's armor, fully accessorized. As God's special forces, outfitted to stand our ground, we must be clothed in Christ.

But God knows a suit of armor over our street clothes won't do. I expect contemporary armor is made of more high-tech fabric: super strong and super pliable but lightweight, with a snug fit for good aerodynamics. Clothing ourselves in Christ would be more like slipping into our Under Armour, not only formfitting but also warm and weather-resistant. Sure, it's a bit of a stretch to get it on, but it's the elasticity that makes it a perfect fit. In the armor of Christ, I am so strong on the inside, I don't need to armor up on the outside. With strength like that, I can do anything.

Activity

Stretch to strengthen using the "Spirit of the Living God" video. Resistance bands are a safe, low-cost, versatile tool for stretching and strengthening. Use a band (they are available in easy, moderate, strong, or superstrong resistance levels and also available latex-free) and follow the choreography in the video performed to the song "Spirit of the Living God." (See https://upperroombooks.com/madetomove.) If you do not have resistance bands, you may use a hand towel or necktie, or simply fold your hands together loosely, making a loop with your arms.

- For maximum effectiveness, keep the band taut throughout the movement routine.
    Spirit of the living God,
    fall afresh on me.
    Spirit of the living God,
    fall afresh on me.
    Melt me, mold me,
    fill me, use me.
    Spirit of the living God,
    fall afresh on me.
    (UMH, no. 393)
- Repeat several times. Pray and listen with your body as you move.
  — Move slowly, attending to how your body feels as you move with the rhythm and in time with the phrasing. Meet your body here.
  — Listen carefully to the words and how you are expressing them in and with your body. Pray with your body.
  — Feel your body stretched by the band and meet that stretch with the strength of your muscles. Move your body and let it move you.
  — Option: If you wish to increase the intensity of movement, stretch the band farther or press in mini-pulses at the end of each phrase.
  — How did you feel? Stretched? Strengthened? Both?

Reflection

- Life is a progressive training plan. We grow into maturity as we stretch day by day. Sometimes things that stretch us make us stronger. Sometimes strong or forceful things stretch us. Which seems particularly true in your life right now? Are you growing stronger? more flexible? both?

- If God called you to battle right now, who or what would be your strength? Sketch a picture of yourself clothed in your super suit.
- Clothed in Christ, fitted with the power of God, what can you do? What is God preparing you to do?

Prayer

Mighty and powerful God, thank you for sending Jesus, clothed in human flesh, so that I might be clothed in Christ. Remind me to take the time to be clothed in you so that, whatever I face, we face together. When I'm afraid, remind me that I can do all things through Christ who strengthens me. Amen.

Friday, Week 5

Love Your Neighbors, All Your Neighbors

Read Matthew 5:43-48.

> "You have heard that it was said, 'You shall love your neighbor and hate your enemy.' But I say to you, Love your enemies and pray for those who persecute you, so that you may be children of your Father in heaven; for he makes his sun rise on the evil and on the good, and sends rain on the righteous and on the unrighteous."
>
> —Matthew 5:43-45

It's easy to love the people I like a lot. But those other people—the ones who by hostility and opposition have made them my enemies—are really a challenge. Yet Jesus says love even them.

How am I going to love and pray for them? It is a command, so I pray, "Lord, I lift _____ to you." But the moment I speak their names before God, all the feelings I've been harboring against my enemies come rushing in. Feelings of anger, hate, fear, shame, guilt, insecurity, disgust, remorse, and pride. As it turns out, praying for my enemy shows me a truth about myself: In the presence of my enemy, I become my own enemy. I must pray for that!

God is not satisfied to brush feelings aside. God wants to get to the bottom of our hearts, down to the places where the light of love hasn't shown in a while. So when I name in prayer the enemies who have done me harm, God doesn't just deal with them, God deals with me. All at once, a light shines on the truth I don't want to face: I don't like the me I see when they behave that way! God invites me to lift those feelings to God. The way I feel about my enemies comes between God and me, and those feelings are too heavy to hold.

The heart is lightened when we hand over to God what we didn't realize we'd been clenching. Leavened with love and forgiveness, we are set free to love all our neighbors sincerely.

Activity

- Option 1: Think about your hard-to-love neighbor as you exercise (walk, run, cycle, move) today. What does God show you about him/her? What does God show you about yourself?
- Option 2 or during cool down: Perform the Lord's Prayer neck stretch. Yesterday, we stretched to strengthen in prayer. Today, we'll stretch to pray for our enemies as Jesus taught us. Using the video, perform the Lord's Prayer "Neck Stretch." (See https://upperroombooks.com/madetomove.)

> Our Father, who art in heaven,
> hallowed be thy name,
> thy kingdom come
> thy will be done
> on earth as it is in heaven.
>
> Give us this day, our daily bread.
> Forgive us our trespasses
> as we forgive those who trespass against us.
> Lead us, not into temptation,
> but deliver us from evil.
>
> For thine is the kingdom,

and the power,
and the glory,
forever. Amen.

- Make a prayer card (4 x 6 index card or similar). In the center, draw a simple illustration characterizing how God "appears" to you in this life season. At each of the four corners, write a prayer category. Sample categories could include the following: (1) friends and family, (2) vocation/work/service, (3) world, and (4) enemies. Pencil in details in each corner according to category. Under enemies, list those things or feelings that you find unlikable in your enemy and/or in yourself when you pray for an enemy.
- Use the list on your prayer card to pray for your enemy. As you pray, it may be helpful to begin with, "Father, forgive them for they know not what they do." Or "Father, forgive me, for I know not what I do." Welcome the forgiveness offered in Christ.
- As you make peace with what you have listed, or as prayers are answered, erase them from your card.

Reflection

- We have a model for forgiveness in this: "While we were yet sinners, Christ died for us" (Rom. 5:8). If loving your enemies feels like it will just kill you, you're one with Christ, our Savior. Who is your enemy? How did it feel to pray *for* your enemy?
- Loving our neighbors as ourselves sets us on a course to befriend them. What stands in the way of befriending yourself? How about your enemy? Can you pray for a changed heart in yourself? In your enemy?
- How well do you know your neighbors? What can you do to get to know them better? How can you include your neighbors—all neighbors—in your circle of fellowship? Could you visit them? Organize a block party? Invite them for a meal? Other?
- How can you open your door to allow Christ to open a door for them?

Prayer

Merciful God, thank you for meeting me everywhere, even in the darkest places of my own soul, for I cannot love myself or love others without tending to those places in me. Forgive me, Lord, for putting those things between us. What a joy it is to draw nearer to you than I ever dreamed possible. In the warmth of your love, let me draw ever nearer to all those whom you love. Amen.

Saturday, Week 5

When Love Comes Calling

Read Matthew 14:22-32.

> Immediately Jesus reached out his hand and caught [Peter]. "You of little faith," he said, "why did you doubt?"
>
> —Matthew 14:31 (NIV)

Good grief! Who in the world supposes they can walk on water? Where do you step? How do you keep your balance? How do you *not* notice the wind? But this is Peter, the disciple who regularly tosses good sense aside and dives right in. (See John 21:4-8 and Mark 9:2-8.) Back in the boat, the rest of the disciples are probably thinking, *There goes Peter off the deep end again.* But Peter doesn't give it a second thought; his Lord is calling him. "Here I come!"

True love does this to us. Love is more than an emotion; it sets us in motion. When someone we love calls, we come running without hesitation or second thought. Nothing else matters. But how the windy world can distract us. It shouts, "You can't walk on water! You're not even a good swimmer! What were you thinking?" As soon as doubt and fear enter our minds, we start believing them. In an instant, the love that moments ago made water-walking a cinch now dims in the distance. When our feet start to sink below the waves, we cry out, "Lord, save me!"

Why does Jesus invite us to come? So he can save us! And not just to take us to heaven but to free us from our fear and doubt. Jesus knows we'll only get so far before our uncertainties start to pull us under, so he stays near enough to haul us back aboard if we start to sink. Soaking wet but safely back in the boat, we worship our Savior because now we know he *is* the Son of God. He didn't just save us from death; he brought us to life. That's what love does.

Activity

- Which foot would you use to step out of the boat? Let's find out. Find a flat, open space where you can "fall forward" and catch yourself by stepping out. Stand with your weight evenly distributed on both feet, and gently lean forward until one foot steps out to catch you before you fall. Please do not let yourself fall!
- How did it feel to step out in this way? Did you think about which foot to fall on, or did you react strictly reflexively?
- When we are unsure, we may hesitate and test the waters with our toe. When we are confident, we jump right in. If you saw Jesus walking out on the dark water, what would you do? (Test the water, take a step, jump in with both feet, remain safely on the boat, something else?) Why?

Reflection

- When opportunity calls, how do you tend to respond? Do you think about it? Research? Ask others for opinions? Pray? Wait and see? See what others are doing? Dive right in? Other?
- Jesus told Peter to "Come." (See Matthew 14:29.) Movement is a learning language. How might movement or taking action help you identify a calling?
- When love calls to us, we often act without thinking. Who or what in your life calls this love response out of you?
- If the love of God is not just a noun or an adjective but also a verb, how are you putting God's love into motion?

Prayer

Lord, if that's you telling me to come to you walking on the water, help me take courage and come running. Let me toss off my inhibitions and deny any distraction so I can run across my life as if its trials are just so many waves that you command. Lord, there is no one I love like I love you. Amen.

6

Body Renewed

He who was seated on the throne said, "Behold, I am making all things new." Also he said, "Write this down, for these words are trustworthy and true."

—Revelation 21:5 (ESV)

God is living and active in our days and in our lives, making all things new. This week, let us uncover the new things God is doing as we offer ourselves, willingly and completely.

Sunday, Week 6

Revealing a New Thing

Read John 20:24-29.

> Thomas (who was called the Twin), one of the twelve, was not with them when Jesus came. So the other disciples told him, "We have seen the Lord." But he said to them, "Unless I see the mark of the nails in his hands, and put my finger in the mark of the nails and my hand in his side, I will not believe."
>
> —John 20:24-25

When something seems too good to be true, it usually is. This had to be what Thomas, the doubting disciple, was thinking when he distrusted the testimony of his fellow disciples. A few Jesus sightings weren't enough for him. He needed to confirm the evidence by the testimony of his own senses, to see and touch in order to believe.

Our earthly bodies are more than containers for an earthly life, they're incubators for an abundant life. Over the course of a lifetime, our physical nature provides a touchstone for the One who created and formed us, who redeems us and calls us by name.

Thank God for Thomas, the patriarch of kinesthetic Christians! By his conviction, we get a glimpse of the resurrected Christ, not just revived or resuscitated, not come back to a life already in progress, but raised to *new* life. When this was revealed to Thomas, there was no room for doubt. "My Lord and my God!" (John 20:28).

When the risen Christ is revealed to us, the full power of the Resurrection is released in us. Our Lord doesn't just lay claim to our spiritual nature, but to our physical nature as well: heart, soul, mind, and strength! It's no wonder Jesus says to love God with each of these. (See Matthew 22:37.) We need our entire selves to love God fully. Kinesthetic Christians need more than hearsay; we need to get physical. We need to go, do, and see for ourselves.

Activity

- Close your eyes and imagine being with Thomas and the others in the closed room when a man resembling the Lord Jesus came and stood among them saying, "Peace be with you." Put yourself in this place.
- Become aware of the room, the people, the place, the feeling in the room. What do your senses tell you? What do you see, hear, smell, taste, touch?
- The man who has come looks at you in love and motions for you to come. You move nearer and then, showing you his hands and his side, he invites you to reach out your hand and touch his wounds. What do you do? How does this feel?
- Bring yourself back to the present, to this moment. Illustrate the scene you have just witnessed. Use pencils, pens, paints, crayons, or other media. Use color or shades of gray.

Reflection

- Sit with the image you have created. Practice being in the presence of the risen Christ.
- What feelings does it evoke? Allow all feelings: external and internal sensation, physical manifestation, and emotional response. Honor them without denial or dismissal.
- Are you in the picture you have created? If not, where are you?
- Recreate this image from the omniscient perspective, as one looking upon the whole scene from above or outside of it.
- What does the Lord show you from the new perspective?

Prayer:

Lord God, forgive me for the times I have been reluctant to believe and even downright difficult. You know that I sometimes need extra convincing. In these times, I am especially thankful for the doubting disciple, Thomas. He gives me hope on the days when I am uncertain and sustains my hope for others, even those who do not yet believe. You are always doing a new thing. Help me to perceive it. Amen.

Monday, Week 6

A New and Willing Heart

Read Ezekiel 36:1-38.

> A new heart I will give you, and a new spirit I will put within you; and I will remove from your body the heart of stone and give you a heart of flesh.
>
> —Ezekiel 36:26

Remember the Grinch? He hated the whole Christmas season, and no one quite knew the reason. Some thought it was because his head wasn't screwed on quite right, and others thought it was because his shoes were too tight. But they agreed that the most likely explanation was that his heart was two sizes too small.

Have you ever known a Grinch or perhaps even been one—a bit greedy, grumpy, jealous, mean-spirited, or small-hearted? The good news is that all hearts have growth potential. Challenged in healthy ways to pump a little harder or a little faster, hearts do grow —not necessarily in size but in capability. A conditioned heart delivers more blood with each beat. Even "broken" hearts can grow new vessels to restore blood flow where it is needed.

When God promises a new heart to Ezekiel and the people of Israel, rather than just replacing their hearts, God makes improvements. "A new heart I will give you, and a new spirit I will put within you; and I will remove from your body the heart of stone and give you a heart of flesh" (Ezek. 36:26). In place of the granite that would last for centuries, God puts flesh that would only last a lifetime, but it could beat. Only a beating heart can respond, not only to challenge, hardship, and heavy demands but also to opportunity, inspiration, and awe. Our hearts are made to come to life.

So, according to Dr. Suess, the holiday spirit of the Whos down in Whoville caused that grinchy heart to grow three sizes on Christmas Day. And then "when the true meaning of Christmas came through, the Grinch found the strength of ten Grinches, plus two!"* When we offer our willing heart, isn't it amazing what God can do?

Activity

- Place your hand over your heart. Can you feel it beating? (If this is difficult, you may wish to feel your carotid pulse (at the side of your neck) or your radial pulse (at your wrist).
- By now, you know your grab bag well. Lay all the options out in front of you.
- Which are your favorites? Which will you keep doing? Which one will you do today?
- Do it. Pause midway and notice your pulse. Speak your thanks in rhythm for the heart God began beating in you. Listen for God's response to your good stewardship on behalf of God's creation.

Reflection

- What does it mean to love God with your whole heart?
- What has changed in you as you have attempted to love God with all of your heart?
- What does the beating of your heart suggest about the nature or character of God?

Prayer

Thank you, God, for my heart, the magnificent organ that serves with such humility to distribute my life's blood. Help me to care for it well so I can use it to respond to the needs of my world and to your calling on my life. Father, you always know best. Amen.

*Dr. Seuss, *How the Grinch Stole Christmas!* (New York: Random House, 1957).

Tuesday, Week 6

A New and Willing Soul

Read Ephesians 3:18-21.

> I pray that you may have the power to comprehend, with all the saints, what is the breadth and length and height and depth, and to know the love of Christ that surpasses knowledge, so that you may be filled with all the fullness of God.
>
> —Ephesians 3:18-19

Sometimes, when I look at today's world, I throw my hands up in distress. *What hope do we have when people behave like that?* Yet discord and strife are nothing new. Dissension has always been with us. Humankind has its shortcomings; the human condition is the mud we're mired in. It's why Christ came and why he died. God knew we would be in desperate need of a Savior.

As Jesus took his last breath on the cross, we breathed our first. Just as God breathes new life into Adam, Christ breathes new hope into our lives. In gratitude we sing:

Breathe on me breath of God. Fill me with life anew,
that I may love what thou dost love, and do what thou wouldst do.
(UMH, no. 420)

Lord, it is your breath in our lungs—the wind of your Spirit, the Holy Spirit of creation—that is ever recreating us. In our believing, we are given new birth into a living hope.

Now in our days, our every breath can remind us God is near. With Paul we humbly ask, "May [I/we] have the power to comprehend, with all the saints, what is the breadth and length and height and depth, and to know the love of Christ that surpasses knowledge, so that [I/we] may be filled with all the fullness of God" (Eph. 3:18-19).

In Christ, we are the hope of a needy world. Even when we tremble upon a precipice or hesitate before a narrow way, may we inhale deeply of God's assurance. There is no fear in a love like that.

Activity

- Slowly and deeply, inhale and then exhale. Repeat, paying special attention to the sensation of your breath.
- Recall your breath prayer and offer it, slowly and gently, pausing briefly but intentionally between inhale and exhale. Focus that moment on what you breathe in and what you breathe out. What thoughts arise? What feelings? What emotions?
- Let the breath of God reach to the depths of your soul. Trust God with whatever is there. Listen for God's response. Thank God for the promise of cleansing, re-creation, and renewal.

Reflection

- What does it mean to love God with your whole soul?
- What has changed in you as you have attempted to love God with all your soul?
- What does the nature of the breath suggest about the character of God? of God's Holy Spirit?

Prayer

Jesus, Lord of my life, you prepared a way for me before I was born and bring life to me daily. Stay close to me, I pray. Let me feel your love both in the soft breeze and the gale force winds, a love that transcends earthly rivalries and bridges all differences, a love like no other. May it unite all humankind so we may be one, as you and the Father and the Spirit are one. Amen.

Wednesday, Week 6

A New and Willing Mind

Read Romans 12:1-7.

> Therefore, I urge you, brothers and sisters, in view of God's mercy, to offer your bodies as a living sacrifice, holy and pleasing to God—this is your true and proper worship. Do not conform to the pattern of this world, but be transformed by the renewing of your mind. Then you will be able to test and approve what God's will is—his good, pleasing and perfect will.

> —Romans 12:1-2 (NIV)

We do some things without really thinking, like write our name, comb our hair, walk, run, or ride a bike. These things don't require full attention because they've become second nature to us. Other things we do out of habit, like having morning coffee, turning on the TV after dinner, checking our phone for notifications, or choosing the same seat in class or the same pew each Sunday at church. We are aware we do these things, but they've become automatic. The human animal is a creature of habit, though some habits, particularly those that aren't good for us, can be very difficult to break.

But there's hope. God knew that life would be habit-forming and made us this way so our brains wouldn't be completely occupied with the simple mechanics of living. Just imagine if we had to consciously direct every muscle in every motion and respond to every sound and every sensation all day, every day. We could attend to nothing else! Thus, God created us with brains able to delegate the basics to our subconscious, leaving room to set our minds on higher things.

But minds and bodies are not separate entities, competing to take charge of our lives. They work together as a unit in order to coordinate a healthy, full life. Our minds, acting CEOs for our body's physical, mental, social, and emotional demands, are so much more than hardwired computing devices. They are living organs, continuously reconfiguring connections according to their surroundings, circumstances, and environment. Yes, in many ways, we are what we think. Surely this is why Paul advises, "Do not conform to the pattern of this world, but be transformed by the renewing of your mind" (Rom. 12:2, NIV).

Makes you think, doesn't it?

Activity

- Find a place that is stillness for you. Perhaps it is a quiet room, a sunny porch, a babbling brook, a mountain view. Find a special place where you and God can be alone together.
- Sit in this stillness and try to imagine the mind of God that conceived of you on the day God created you. Ask the Spirit of God to take you back and back, deep and deeper.
- Take Christ's hand in this place and walk together into the present. Match your footsteps to his. Focus your mind and attention on your companion, and move at his pace. No matter how fast or slow you go, it will be stillness for you if your gaze is fixed on Christ.

Reflection

- What does it mean to love God with your whole mind?
- What has changed in you as you have attempted to love God with your whole mind?
- What does the working of your mind suggest about the nature or character of God?

Prayer

O God, though my thoughts are not your thoughts and my ways are not your ways, you do not give up on me. Open my mind to you and direct my every thought. Let your thoughts become my thoughts and your ways become my ways as your will becomes my way forward. Amen.

Thursday, Week 6

The Master Bodybuilder

Read 1 Corinthians 12:12-27.

> Now you are the body of Christ and individually members of it.
>
> —1 Corinthians 12:27

How do you build a body? For a competitive bodybuilder, it's a full-time occupation. They spend hours in the gym, carving those rippling muscles, but it's not just about pumping iron. To develop the highly defined, perfectly symmetrical musculature that will impress the judges, they must carefully control nutrition and hydration to maximize presentation. Bodybuilders are sculpting themselves into living works of art.

Each of us is a work of art living a life that requires a whole-body effort. Though we're not trying to impress judges with our bulging muscles, God does expect us to be working out. Each of us, as members together in the body of Christ, have been apportioned gifts to develop and display. Size is of no consequence, but definition is essential. God, as master bodybuilder, is sculpting this body to achieve perfect proportions. We, as building blocks—living stones—are being built into a spiritual house. (See 1 Peter 2:4-5.) Whoever we are and whatever we do, God is on display.

In order for the body of Christ that God is building to be absolutely flawless, every contribution is essential. Our merciful God has provided special dispensation for weaker and less honorable body parts. God takes special care in covering them because if one part suffers, the whole body suffers with it. When the whole body works together for the good of those whom God loves, we don't just look good; we shine with God's glory. No one can compete with that.

Activity

- Find a public place where many people gather. Perhaps it is a church, a market, a library, or a bus station. Maybe it is a school or your workplace.
- Look around at all the people. Notice the variety of sizes and shapes; colors and hues; ways of dressing, speaking, and behaving. Take a moment to marvel at all the different expressions of our creative God. Which of the people resembles you? Are there any who are exactly like you?
- As you go through your day, use your strength wherever you are able. Forgo the automatic in favor of good old-fashioned human power. Wherever you are able, lift, push, carry, or pull. Decline assistance if you can do it yourself, and offer assistance to those who may need it. In thanks for the body God gave you, use it!

Reflection

- What does it mean to love God with all your strength?
- What has been changed in you as you have attempted to love God with all your strength?
- What does the nature of the body of Christ suggest to you about the character of God?

Prayer

God, to know that you are sculpting me as part of the body of Christ is nearly impossible to fathom. What a privilege, and what a responsibility. Let this promise and this honor motivate me to work my hardest to develop the gifts you have given particularly to me. Let my efforts express my gratitude so that my offering may be pleasing and acceptable to you. Amen.

Friday, Week 6

Firm Footing Lets Us Leap with Joy

Read Psalm 18.

> You gave me a wide place for my steps under me,
>   and my feet did not slip.

—Psalm 18:36

Have you ever watched a toddler learning to walk? They fall a lot. Children are wobbly on their feet until they get their balance. Learning to work arms, legs, and torso together is hard. We may be tempted to hover over them to prevent them from falling, but teetering, toppling, and getting back up is how they develop the strength and coordination they need to find their footing. If they rely on our strength, they don't develop their own. The best way to help a new walker is to remove all the impediments and soften the landing. They're going to fall.

Could this be why God sometimes lets us fall, so we can learn to stand up and walk? God knows the balance, strength, and resilience we'll need to negotiate the life that lies ahead of us. It will be full of stumbling blocks. But we're not made just to stand; we're made to walk, run, and leap for joy. Perhaps this is why we find such joy watching children learn to navigate the playground, and we delight when they leap with glee into the lake.

Unfortunately, falls do still happen. Surfaces can be slippery, and footing can be treacherous. If the dock you are standing on isn't secured, that leap won't take you far. Footing and stability are as important as strength and power if you want to make a big splash with that cannonball. But when we are centered, confident, and firmly grounded in Christ, we can leap farther than we ever thought possible and splash with tremendous exuberance. Imagine the joy that must give our heavenly Parent.

Activity

   (See https://upperroombooks.com/madetomove.)
   - How flexible are you? Let's try again to do the sit-and-reach stretch that we tried on the Friday of Week 1. Can you reach your toes now? If you have been practicing, you should be closer. Reach and hold this stretch, using the assist to pull you forward if you need it.
   - Try this challenge if you are able: "Invert" the sit and reach. Lie on the floor with your hips pushed as close as possible to the base of the wall, and extend your legs straight up, resting your heels against the wall. Pause, exhale fully, and let yourself be stretched.
   - How does it feel when you release the stretch? Try the sit-and-reach stretch again. Can you stretch further?

Reflection

   - What does it mean to love your neighbor as yourself? To love your whole neighborhood? How does loving your neighbor as yourself stretch you?
   - What has been changed in you as you have allowed God to stretch you?
   - What does God's "life-stretching program" suggest about the character of God?

Prayer

Lord, thank you. Each time I fall, you help me to my feet again, stronger each time I rise. You are the strength at my center and the foundation of my footing. Please show me those who may need a hand. When I reach for them, let your strength be the strength I rely on and your power be the power they perceive. You are my rock and my Redeemer. I am ever grateful that you will never be moved. Amen.

Saturday, Week 6

Set Free for a Life of Abundance

Read John 10:7-10.

> Jesus said again, "Very truly I tell you, I am the gate for the sheep."
>
> —John 10:7 (NIV)

The good thing about telling the truth, I've been told, is that you can always tell it again. Lies, on the other hand, are a moving target. They find us out in the end. It's better to start with what's right and stick to it. As Jesus said, "If you hold to my teaching, you are really my disciples. Then you will know the truth, and the truth will set you free" (John 8:31-32).

On Saturday of Week 1 of our study, we acknowledged the "guardrails of life" that God provides for us in anticipation of our early-learning stumbles. But as we mature, we learn to walk without holding on. As we gain confidence, we manage to keep our balance even while running. In our race toward the finish line, we must stay in our lanes even on the tightest of turns or risk disqualification.

For mature members of the household of God, the guardrails come down, but the standards go up. Beyond simply conforming to the rules and regulations of everyday life, we must comply with the highest of standards, in accordance with the love and self-discipline the Spirit of God gave us. That's where our power comes from—the power to resist evil and injustice and to act on what is good and right. The Word of God trains us in righteousness, and we are thoroughly equipped for every good work. (See 2 Timothy 3:17.)

When the storms of life threaten to knock us off course, God doesn't want us to cower in fear. God wants us to spring to life, the abundant life Christ came to give us. But the abundant life cannot be lived in confinement; it needs room to roam. Emboldened by the truth and secure in the love and acceptance of Christ, we can venture into life's wilderness free of fear and "confident of this, that he who began a good work in you will carry it on to completion until the day of Christ Jesus" (Phil. 1:6, NIV).

Activity

- Even the neatest of people have a messy place, where odds and ends pile up when we don't get around to cleaning. What or where is your messy place?
- Today, tackle one such place. Give the effort to God. Together, decide what needs keeping, what needs tossing, and what needs to go elsewhere or to someone else.
- How did the cleanup go? How does the formerly messy place feel to you now?

Reflection

- What does it mean to love God with your whole self?
- How does living in obedience to God free us for a more abundant life?
- What does the life of Jesus, our Good Shepherd, reveal to us about the nature of God?

Prayer

Loving and all-powerful God, from the very first you knew who I would be and what it would take to get me there. Thank you for sending Jesus to show me the way. Propel me in your direction. Free me from anything that holds me back and remind me of anything I'm meant to bring along. Let's get going together! Amen.

7

Body Alive

Since, then, you have been raised with Christ, set your hearts on things above, where Christ is, seated at the right hand of God.

—Colossians 3:1 (NIV)

Living a life that seeks to know and love God fully prepares us for the journey and provides us with what we will need to arrive safely. Trusting this, what will you do with what the love of Christ has brought to life in you?

Sunday, Week 7

Eat, Drink, and Come to Life

Read John 14:1-7.

> "Do not let your hearts be troubled. Believe in God, believe also in me."
>
> —John 14:1

Our tour leaders for the five-day bicycling excursion were not only exceedingly fit but also incredibly well prepared. After breakfast each morning, they hosted "route wrap," describing our ride for the day in detail. They assured us that a support van would transport our belongings to the next inn and these items would be waiting for us in our rooms when we arrived; all we had to do was get ourselves to the next inn. But between here and there would be some "rolls" and some long, winding climbs. "Vermont ain't flat," our leaders warned. "Just remember: Eat before you're hungry, and drink before you're thirsty."

Because life has a habit of sapping our energy and leaving us hungry and thirsty at the end of the day, this is mighty good advice. We'd do well to prepare ourselves with solid sustenance. Jesus offers himself. "I am the bread of life. Whoever comes to me will never be hungry, and whoever believes in me will never be thirsty" (John 6:35). He provides the bread and living water to go with it, not a fountain of youth but a source of replenishment that will never run dry.

Thanks to our tour leaders who supplied snacks and water-bottle refills along the way, we were able to reach the summits and enjoy the exhilarating mountaintop vistas, satisfied with our cycling accomplishments. But I must confess that, after a day of sweating steep ascents, holding my breath through perilous descents, rattling over railroad crossings and the washboard of unpaved roads, there was nothing quite as welcome as the sight of the next inn in the distance. It held the promise of food, beverage, and the good company of other travelers around the supper table. The innkeeper was always waiting to greet us and show us to our rooms.

Life ain't flat. Our job is just to get ourselves to the inn. Best of all, a place has been prepared. Our room is ready.

Activity

- Rest.
- Who has been a tour leader or guide for your life's climb thus far? Offer a prayer of thanks for that person. If he or she is still alive, send a note or give the person a call to express your thanks. If the person has died, perhaps you can send a note to the person's family, sharing what his or her life meant to you.
- Read Isaiah 55. Consider these verses in your mind's eye:

> For you shall go out in joy,
>   and be led back in peace;
> the mountains and the hills before you
>   shall burst into song,
>   and all the trees of the field shall clap their hands.
> Instead of the thorn shall come up the cypress;
>   instead of the brier shall come up the myrtle;
> and it shall be to the LORD for a memorial,
>   for an everlasting sign that shall not be cut off.
> —Isaiah 55:12-13

- Imagine receiving the ovation of nature itself. What is your view from this mountaintop?
- God has provided a place for you at the inn. How will your life express your thanks?

Prayer

Wonderful Creator, Magnificent Provider, Holy Redeemer, Incarnate God, thank you for providing all that I need and being all that I need. You are my bread and water, the body and blood of my life. Teach me to love the image of you that is created uniquely in me. By your grace, let me live a life that allows your love to show. A life that is truly life. Amen.

Conclusion

I Am Yours

But now thus says the LORD,
    he who created you, O Jacob,
    he who formed you, O Israel:
Do not fear, for I have redeemed you;
    I have called you by name, you are mine.

—Isaiah 43:1

Dear, God, who are you? Where are you? Lord, I listen, but I can't hear you. I want to know you. I want to thank you. Come, please come and be with me now. Assure me you'll be with me always.

In response to our plea, the Lord offers us the simplest of instructions. *Love. Love me with all your heart and all your soul and all your mind and all your strength. And love your neighbor as yourself. Do this, and you will live,* Jesus says. (See Luke 10:25-37.)

Can we do this? Can we love completely? Sometimes it is so hard to take hold of love. We are real, live, tangible human beings. Love is a wonderful idea, but how do we make it real? How can we bring love to life?

Two thousand years ago there lived a young woman whose name was Mary, who must have been completely perplexed to receive the news that she, though an unmarried virgin, would conceive in her womb and bear a son. Yet she believed that what was conceived in her was from the Holy Spirit; this child, Jesus, would be holy.

Each of us, every child born of God, is born to be holy. We embrace this holiness when with Mary we say, *Here I am, the servant of the Lord; let it be with me according to your word. Show me how to love. Help me live in love. I want to give birth to love.* At that moment, love is no longer just a concept or a nice idea. It conceives. It starts to develop and take shape in us. What is conceived in us is from the Holy Spirit. We can give it life.

When my daughter was small, I used to sing her to sleep using the last stanza of the Christmas carol "Away in a Manger."

> Be near me Lord Jesus, I ask thee to stay
> close by me forever, and love me I pray;
> bless all the dear children in thy tender care,
> and fit us for heaven, to live with thee there.
> (UMH, no. 217)

"Fit us for heaven. . . ." My, how our earthly efforts at fitness or fitting in can often feel like competing for survival. Fitting us for heaven is something else entirely. As we learn to love God with all that we are, not only do we become more fit but we become better fit. As we put on the nature of Christ, which is love, we find our fit in and for the kingdom of God breaking in among us.

Though at first we may not be very good at this (we are children, after all), like most things in life, the more we practice, the better we get. During this six-week journey together, we've gotten a lot of practice. While trying to love God in our humanness is enlivening and rejuvenating, it is also hard and can be quite humbling. How good it is to know that we are a work in progress, being aged and refined by a master craftsman who knows just what we'll be. I like to think of us as well water Jesus is turning into fine wine. That's going to take some time!

Our challenge, as Christians who are made to move, is to "lay aside every weight and the sin that clings so closely, and let us run with perseverance the race that is set before us, looking to Jesus the pioneer and perfecter of our faith" (Heb. 12:1-2). We're not here to run somebody else's race but the race *marked out for us*, the one for which we are uniquely qualified, yet constantly being prepared, equipped, and trained.

Of course, we know that in any race there is only one winner, but we need not compete for that prize; it has already been awarded. The rest of us run for the finisher's medal awarded to everyone who crosses the finish line of faith. The baton is in our hands. May we run with perseverance the race of our lives.

Thank you, Magnificent God, for the body that you created uniquely for me. It was you who formed my inward parts and knit me together in my mother's womb. I praise you for I am fearfully and wonderfully made. Grow in me a complete trust that in you I live and move and have my being. Let love make me fully alive. Amen.

Leader's Guide

Made to Move: Knowing and Loving God Through Our Bodies

Just then a lawyer stood up to test Jesus. "Teacher," he said, "what must I do to inherit eternal life?" He said to him, "What is written in the law? What do you read there?" He answered, "You shall love the Lord your God with all your heart, and with all your soul, and with all your strength, and with all your mind; and your neighbor as yourself." And he said to him, "You have given the right answer; do this, and you will live."

—Luke 10:25-28

We are meant to put Jesus' instructions into action. This devotional workbook is a daily guide to help you use your created body—physical, mental, emotional, and spiritual—to know and love God better. I have included the *Made to Move* Leaders Guide to enhance the experience for individuals in classes or small groups who desire to meet together weekly to share what they've learned and to learn from each other.

Because the *Made to Move* approach to the Christian life will be a new approach for many, I have included additional group activities in this guide to enhance your time together. I hope you'll come to each meeting with an open mind and a playful spirit. And be ready to move, because that's the way God made us.

I pray that in your activities, discussions, and sharing, God will be present in new and enlivening ways that you can take with you everywhere you take your body, which is, of course, everywhere you go. To life!

Sample Weekly Meeting Format

Main Message: a summary of the week's theme.

Warm Up: a theme-related activity to get the group started.

Part I: The Workout

Review the meditations from this week. What do they teach you about you? About God?

- Experience—Review our individual daily devotional experiences for the week. Look at the scriptures, meditations, and activities. Which ones most engaged you?
- Insight—From reflection questions, what is God showing you?
- Expand—Share how God is using the physical nature God created in you to connect you to your world, to others, and to yourself.

Part II: The Stretch

Let's go further with these questions. Where is God stretching you or showing you more?

- Question 1 (Q1)—This is a weekly group activity meant to spark conversation about the week's work.
- Question 2 (Q2)—Where is God getting your attention?
- Question 3 (Q3)—Where is God calling you further?

Pep Talk: After discussion and sharing, how will you challenge yourself this week?

High Five: Closing prayer, joys and concerns

Game Plan: Introductory Meeting

Opening questions for group: What do we know about God? Where do we find evidence of God? How are we God's evidence?

Main Message: The one thing we know God gave us just for this lifetime is our human form, our physical bodies. If God wants to be known by us, then our bodies are our nearest, most intimate, most personal, and most accessible means of this revelation.

Warm Up

- Welcome and introductions, see active options below
- Activity (ice breaker, bonding, opener)

> Option 1. Statue Tag: One person is stationed at the light switch. The object for all participants is to move toward the person who is "it" and be the first to tag them without being caught moving. To play: with lights out, everyone is free to move. When lights come on, if you're caught moving, you're out.

> Option 2. Darkness to Light: Keep the lights out for initial class introductions. Describe yourself before telling your name. Lights on—surprise? Hear the voice before seeing the person. Reactions?

- Read aloud Genesis 1, John 1:1-5. Can we see God? How does God make God's self known?
- Respond to the *Made to Move* Introduction. What does it mean to be made to move? To know and love God?

Game Plan, Week 1

Body Image

Main Message

The design reveals the hand of the designer. We are drafted in intricate detail but are not God's finished product. We are created with room to grow.

Warm Up

- Gathering—Read aloud Genesis 1:26-27 and Psalm 139:1-18
- Activity—Sit to stand/Musical chairs or musical rings

> Begin by sitting still and counting your resting pulse for ten seconds. Breathe quietly for ten seconds.

> Option 1: Sit-to-stand chair squats. Go for thirty seconds, according to group tolerance. Afterward, each one should count their pulse for ten seconds, observe breathing, and compare to resting.

Option 2: Musical chairs. Arrange chairs in two rows, back-to-back. Use one less than the number present. Play music. When music stops, find a seat. The person without a seat is out. Take away one chair. Repeat. Those out should breathe and count pulse. (How does it feel to be out? Rules say there is only one winner.)

Or, play musical rings. Arrange large rings (or hula hoops) in open room space. Move among rings while music plays. Stop in a ring. Each time, remove a ring but keep all players. Game ends with all players squeezing at least part of their body into one ring.

Part I: The Workout

- Experience—Review lessons and activities for this week. Which had the most meaning or left a lasting impression on you? (If no one is forthcoming, consider Sunday/Day 1 activity for "God's construction project.")
- Insight—What did this teach you about you? About God?
- Expand—Does this change how you feel about yourself? About God?

Part II: The Stretch

- Q1—Make two lists with these headings: "The Nature of God" and "The Nature of Me." How do you resemble one another? How do you differ? What things would you like to change? What would you leave the same?
- Q2—What does this exercise show you about you as a creation? About God as Creator?
- Q3—What do you as one created "say/express/display" about the nature of God?

Pep Talk

We are created perfect, yet still being perfected. Some people put an extra candle on birthday cakes to symbolize "one to grow on." Where is God actively shaping, crafting, and growing you?

High Five

Closing, joys and concerns, and prayer.

Game Plan, Week 2

Body of Flesh

Main Message

Temptations persist, but with God I can resist. God gives us resources to resist temptation, but we must keep choosing them. How can we stand up to temptation?

Warm Up

- Gathering and welcome
- Activity

    Option 1: Hungry Hippo. Play the board game, or pair up for a life-size game with one person as the "player" and one as the hungry hippo. (Examples of the game can be found on YouTube.) The one who grabs the most wins.

    Option 2: Earworm activity. Play the musical theme from a familiar song (e.g., the theme from *Gilligan's Island* or *Jeopardy*) and stop in the middle. (See how this comes up again throughout your session!) Mid class, play the song all the way through to its conclusion to help rid earworm, or play a familiar hymn ("Amazing Grace" or "Great Is Thy Faithfulness") to invite God to resonate inwardly. See if that leaves a "Godworm."

Part I: The Workout

- Experience—Recall the lessons and activities from this week. Which had the most meaning? Left an impression? (If no one is forthcoming, consider Monday's activity, what is in your grab bag?)
- Insight—What is calling your attention? "Needs work"? What are you willing to commit to? (We are not one-and-done; avoid the New Year's resolution effect = start fast, quit early.)
- Expand—Were there surprises? About you? About God?

Part II. The Stretch

- Q1—Read Luke 4:1-13 aloud. Temptation is a human problem that even Jesus experienced. It does not make us bad, but may open the door to sin. Share what is most tempting for you.

- Q2—Where does temptation hide? How does it disguise itself?
- Q3—How does God help us unmask temptation and steer clear of it? Are there ways to avoid it or things we can do to resist temptation?

Pep Talk

Read the Lord's Prayer. (See Matthew 6:9-13.) Rise and assume your "perfect posture" against the wall. Recite from memory or display Micah 6:6-8. Return to seats maintaining "perfect posture."

High Five

Closing, joys and concerns, and prayer.

Game Plan, Week 3

Body Broken

Main Message

God made us breakable, for we have this treasure in clay jars. God's prevenient grace designed us with means to respond, repair, and grow the characteristics of life itself. We can call on these resources to seek balance and to right ourselves.

Warm Up

- Gathering and welcome. Read 2 Corinthians 4:7-12.
- Activity

  Option 1: Pin the tail on the sheep or donkey, or pin the beard on Jesus. Blindfold, spin, and navigate toward target.

  Option 2. Gather group in circle with one person in center (blindfolded or with closed eyes) who turns around and around and points to someone in the circle who wins if he/she can answer a Bible trivia question asked.

Part I: The Workout

- Experience—Recall lessons and activities from this week. Which had the most meaning? Left the deepest impression?

- Insight—Were there surprises? (If no one is forthcoming, look at the health wheel from Saturday.) Take time to complete the wheel. Mark scores in the various categories.
- Expand—How are we rolling along on our health wheels? Invite group members to share their health wheels.

Part II: The Stretch

- Q1—Create a chart. Column 1: Your brokenness. Column 2: The world's brokenness. Column 3: God of healing, come to me and to these. . . .
- Q2—We, and all of humanity, are immersed in God's prevenient grace. How is God healing what is broken in you? in those around you?
- Q3—Where is God inclining you to work in/among/with/through the brokenness?

Pep Talk

Repaired things are often stronger once they mature (healed broken bones, positive effects of moderate, well-managed stress, etc.). What giftedness is God growing in you? Where might a former weakness be employed as a strength (i.e., what have you learned from God through brokenness, illness, injury, and disappointment?)

High Five

Closing, joys and concerns, and prayer.

Game Plan, Week 4

Body Bent

Main Message

Under the weight of our humanness, God's discipline heals us and moves us toward wholeness. Opposition can hone our capacity to distinguish God's will and adopt humility that helps us choose God's way.

Warm Up

- Gathering and welcome. Read Mark 2.
- Activity

(See https://upperroombooks.com/madetomove.)

The group forms a circle with a full arm's length between individuals. Stand on one foot. Try a standing quad stretch and/or figure 4 stretch (right and left). How is your balance? Move closer so the circle is smaller. Rest one arm gently on shoulder of person next to you (i.e., right arm resting on right neighbor, pick up left foot). Repeat the stretches on right and the left sides. (Helping cue: distributing your weight improves your balance.)

Part I: The Workout

- Experience—Recall lessons and activities this week. Which had the most meaning? Which left the deepest impression?
- Insight—Consider Thursday's activity, isometrics vs. isotonics. Can you define these? How do these apply in our lives? When does more force not move things?
- Expand—Is there somewhere we need to change our effort or strategy? Where? How?

Part II: The Stretch

- Q1—Read Luke 22: 39-46. What are you bent under the weight of? Spend some time with God in prayer/writing. Finish this prayer: "God, give me courage to _____."
- Q2—What if the answer to prayer is no? What would be "sweating blood" to you?
- Q3—When has prayer felt like a physical practice to you? When have you felt God in prayer? Sensed God near? Felt God distant? Heard God? Received a message or thought from God? What did you do with what God gave/handed you?

Pep Talk

A wider stance distributes the weight when you are standing on holy ground. Form your circle again, stand on one foot, then assume a two-footed stance. Me *and* thee, together, *we* are standing on holy ground. Pray together about an act of service your group might perform together.

High Five

Closing, joys and concerns, and prayer.

Game Plan, Week 5
Body Rebuilt

Main Message
I am God's building project and an essential component of God's building. Breaking down to rebuild is necessary but takes dedicated effort and hard work. Stretching against resistance strengthens.

Warm Up
- Gathering and welcome. Play, sing, or speak "Spirit of the Living God" (UMH, no. 393). Move through the stretchy bands choreography.
- Activity

    Use stretchy bands routine to pray through "Spirit of the Living God." In place of bands, you may use towels, ropes, or ties.
    (See https://upperroombooks.com/madetomove.)

Part I: The Workout
- Experience—Recall lessons and activities from the week. Which had the most meaning? Left deepest impression?
- Insight—Did you try fasting from something? What? Where do you eat your meals? Do you sit at a table? Did you say grace? Did you pray before meals as a child? Share words of prayer?
- Expand—Sabbath rest provides rhythm for our lives. What did allowing extra time this week provide for you?

Part II: The Stretch
- Q1—Read 1 Samuel 17 and Ephesians 6:10-18.
- Q2—Where and/or in whom do you see strength? Flexibility? Compare and contrast strength and flexibility. How are they related? (Extra credit for life sciences buffs: Look at length-tension relationship in human muscle contraction.)
- Q3—How does God use both strength and flexibility (God's and ours)? When you put on your super suit, what are your super powers?

Pep Talk

Read or recite together: "I can do all things through Christ who strengthens me." (Phil. 4:13, KJV). The love of God stretches you to strengthen you. God loves us as we are but too much to leave us this way. If love is a verb, what has Love started moving in you?

High Five

Closing, joys and concerns, and prayer. Discuss group service project ideas or plan.

Game Plan, Week 6

Body Renewed

Note: This week's session may require extra time if you are using it as closing session.

Main Message

God is renewing you day by day. One part at a time, one person at a time, alone and together, God is growing us nearer to God, maturing each of us, making of us a new creation—the union of all things in the body of Christ. (See Ephesians 1:9-10.)
 * Consider how you would fill in these blanks:

- God is renewing me day by day for _____.
- God is setting me free to _____.

Warm Up

Ahead of time, set up (or agree to gather in) a prayer space. Possible spaces include: sanctuary, altar with kneeling pads or spaces, or a regular meeting room but have participants bring towels/mats to kneel on.

- Gathering and welcome. Read Isaiah 43:1-7.
- "Spirit of Living God" prayer stretch.
  (See https://upperroombooks.com/madetomove.)

Part I: The Workout

- Introduce Paul's prayer for the Gentiles found in Ephesians 3:14-19. Have one member of the group read it aloud as Paul. Invite participants to listen as if it is prayed for them.
- Read the prayer again silently, inserting your own name for the bolded "you."
- Experience—Rise and prayer-walk through your meeting space, building, property, neighborhood; take journal, camera, paper and pencil, paints/markers/colored pencils with you to reflect.
- Insight—Ask participants to prepare a summary of their experience to share with the group.
- Expand—Come together at the meeting table to share insights and gleanings.
- Close by reading Ephesians 3:20-21.

Part II: The Stretch

- Q1—What are the insights from this week's lessons and activities?
- Q2—How does it feel to gather with the disciples when the resurrected Christ comes to stand among them? (Reference Sunday's meditation.)
- Q3—What does it mean to:
  — (Monday) love God with a new heart
  — (Tuesday) love God with a new and willing soul
  — (Wednesday) love God with a renewed mind
  — (Thursday) love God with new strength
  — (Friday) love God in your new neighbor
  — (Saturday) be set free to love abundantly?

Pep Talk

Even when you feel like you are wasting away, you are being renewed day by day. What are you growing into? Where is God remodeling you?

High Five

Closing, joys and concerns, prayer. Discuss and finalize plans for serving as a group as introduced at the close of last week's group meeting. Prepare group for closing fellowship celebration at last meeting. Holy Communion for the final group meeting is an option. Make plans to include a clergyperson who can consecrate the elements if you choose this option.

Game Plan, Conclusion

Body Alive

Main Message

What is God's preparation training and equipping you for? What is the race marked out for you?

Warm Up

- Gathering and welcome
- Activity

    Form an archway tunnel with hands to run through, like parents sometimes do at soccer games. Run through the tunnel in partner pairs. The first pair runs through and forms an arch with partner to extend the tunnel for the rest.

Part I: Workout

- Experience—Read Luke 15:11-32 or perform as script and cast of characters: father, brother(s) or brother and sister, field hands/slaves, prodigal's friends, pigs
- Insight—Who are you in this story?
- Expand—What living part are you playing in real life? I am cast as _____ in God's play. Explore this with other members of your group.

Part II: The Stretch

- Recall Deuteronomy 6:4-9 and Luke 10:25-28.
- Think about life as journey or bicycle excursion or tour. Review the meditations from the week. How do we experience the uphills in life? the downhills? the climbs? the valleys? the mountaintops? hunger and thirst? provision? Use large poster paper and allow individuals to draw or annotate the contours of their life's journey. (Option: Use mural paper to overlay the journeys of members of the group, using different colors to distinguish each. Are there commonalities? Differences? What do these say? What are the lessons learned?)
- Q1—Read John 6:25-40. If your group is celebrating Holy Communion, do so at this time.
- Q2—Read Isaiah 55:12-13.

- Q3—Imagine receiving the ovation of nature itself as you arrive. What is your view from this mountaintop?
- Read John 14:1-3. God has provided a place for you at the inn. How will your life express thanks?

Pep Talk

We are made to move, inside, outside, and along the way. Life is a journey. Living a life knowing and loving God prepares us and provides what we need to arrive safely.

High Five

Closing, joys and concerns, and prayer.

Pray together the prayer from Week 7.

Wonderful Creator, Magnificent Provider, Incarnate God, thank you for providing all that I need and being all that I need. You are my bread and water, the body and blood of my life. Teach me to love the image of You that is created uniquely in me. By your grace, let me live a life that lets that love show. A life that is truly life. Amen.

Made to Move for Children

Hear, O Israel: The Lord *is our God, the* Lord *alone. You shall love the* Lord *your God with all your heart, and with all your soul, and with all your might. Keep these words that I am commanding you today in your heart. Recite them to your children and talk about them when you are at home and when you are away, when you lie down and when you rise.*

—Deuteronomy 6:4-7

Jesus said, "You shall love the Lord your God with all your heart, and with all your soul, and with all your mind, and with all your strength.' The second is this, 'You shall love your neighbor as yourself.' There is no other commandment greater than these."

—Mark 12:30-31

Overview

Each week includes:

- scripture emphasis from Deuteronomy 6:4-9, Mark 12:30-31
- supporting theme/message
- reinforcing activity
- Thinking Things
- closing action prayer

Introductory Week—We love because God first loved us. (See 1 John 4:19.)

Week 1—Heart (beating, pumping, working, pace)

Week 2—Soul (breath, rhythm, sensing, inspiration)

Week 3—Mind (brain, memory, understanding, learning)

Week 4—Strength (muscles, energy, movement, growing)

Week 5—Neighbor (flexibility, reaching, outreach, community)

Week 6—My Whole Self (God-made, God-loved, self-care, self-respect, self-disciplined)

Conclusion week—Full of heart, soul, mind, and strength is how God made me and how God made you. Together, we care for ourselves, each other, and all of God's creation.

Introduction week
- Verse: "We love because God first loved us" (1 John 4:19).
- Theme: God loved me even before I was born.
- Activity ideas: Birthday celebration for everyone! Invitations, cards, birth announcements, gifts, cake, party hats. Make a calendar to see when everyone's birthday is. For youth, search for who else was born on your birthday.
- Thinking Things: What do we celebrate on our birthday? What preparations do we make before a birthday celebration? How did God prepare for us to be born?
- Action prayer: (marching) "We love because God first loved us."

Week 1: Heart
Our heart is beating, pumping, working, and help us pace ourselves.

- Verses: "'You shall love the Lord your God *with all your heart*, and with all your soul, and with all your mind, and with all your strength.' The second is this, 'You shall love your neighbor as yourself.' There is no other commandment greater than these" (Mark 12:30-31, author's emphasis).
- Theme: My heartbeat reminds me that God is with me.
- Activity ideas: Feel your heart beating, activity stations to get your heart pumping, running, jumping, hopping, skipping, tip-toeing, etc.) Can you count your heartbeat?
- Thinking things: When does your heart beat faster? Slower? Why do you think God made you that way?
- Action prayer: Jump to familiar chorus or hymn such as: "Yes Lord, yes Lord, yes, yes, Lord" from "I'm Trading My Sorrows" chorus.

Week 2: Soul

Our soul breathes in rhythm, and senses and responds with inspiration and expiration.

- Verses: "'You shall love the Lord your God with all your heart, and *with all your soul*, and with all your mind, and with all your strength.' The second is this, 'You shall love your neighbor as yourself.' There is no other commandment greater than these" (Mark 12:30-31, author's emphasis).
- Theme: My breath helps me "listen for" (or sense/tune in to) God.
- Activity ideas: Deep breaths, shallow breaths, blow out quickly and slowly, making different sounds (whoosh, roar, whistle, whisper, etc.). Write a breath prayer and pray it using your breath. If space allows, do a relaxing meditation calling attention to all parts of the body and asking these parts to relax.
- Thinking Things: Do you breathe when you're sleeping? Why do you "breathe in" (inhale) *and* "breathe out" (exhale)? What does breathing have to do with using your voice? How did meditating feel? What did God show you in the quiet stillness?
- Action prayer: video—"Spirit of the Living God" stretch. (See https://upperroombooks.com/madetomove.)

Week 3: Mind

Our mind's headquarters is the brain where we have memory, understanding, and learning.

- Verses: "'You shall love the Lord your God with all your heart, and with all your soul, and *with all your mind*, and with all your strength.' The second is this, 'You shall love your neighbor as yourself.' There is no other commandment greater than these" (Mark 12:30-31, author's emphasis).
- Theme: God gave me a good mind.
- Activity ideas: Thinking games like concentration, focus on an eye chart, repeat a number backwards, memorize a verse of scripture, find what's missing from a group of items. What do they have in common? What's different? Learn all of the person's names in class. Who can say them all? Draw or color from your imagination: God/Jesus/the Holy Spirit and you. Add family and friends.
- Thinking things: Does God have a mind? How is God's "mind" like yours? How are they different? For youth, *A Wrinkle in Time* has a wonderfully creative plot about a boy's mind used to control a place. Conversation based on the book or the movie would be a great discussion option.
- Action prayer: Pray the Lord's Prayer from memory and do it as a stretch. (See https://upperroombooks.com/madetomove.)

Week 4: Strength

Our strength is in muscles energized to move us, support us, and help us grow.

- Verses: "'You shall love the Lord your God with all your heart, and with all your soul, and with all your mind, and *with all your strength.*' The second is this, 'You shall love your neighbor as yourself.' There is no other commandment greater than these" (Mark 12:30-31, author's emphasis).
- Theme: God made me strong.
- Activity ideas: Find your muscles. Make a fist, bend your elbow, sit and stand, stand on one leg. Children will think of dozens of ways to move using their muscles. Gather things of different weights and see if they can lift them. Have the whole class push on the wall together to see if it moves. For youth, if you think something is heavy and it turns out to be light, you exert way too much force. The way the body prepares muscle fibers for the force anticipated is a fascinating mechanism and great launch for conversation.
- Thinking things: Why does using my muscles make them stronger? Does that make me stronger? Where does my strength come from? What happens if I don't use my muscles? If there is a student with a disability, how is God making them strong? Where is it most difficult to be strong? (Standing up to bullies, doing the right thing, etc.)
- Action prayer: Sing a song with movement, such as, "Head, Shoulders, Knees, and Toes."

Week 5: Neighbor

Neighbors help us be flexible, stretching us to reach out to our community.

- Verses: "'You shall love the Lord your God with all your heart, and with all your soul, and with all your mind, and with all your strength.' The second is this, 'You shall *love your neighbor* as yourself.' There is no other commandment greater than these" (Mark 12:30-31, author's emphasis).
- Theme: God loves my neighbors too!
- Activity ideas: Use Twister game to get kids all tangled up with each other. Getting along together sometimes means discomfort, awkwardness, and stretching! Each child can draw their neighborhood. Label houses, people, pets, etc. Put all the drawings together to make a community. Where is your church in this community? For youth, use a map to look at town, city, state, country, and world. Point out where Jesus' neighborhood would have been on world map. Teens are often surprised by how small Israel is.

- Thinking things: What does being a good neighbor mean? Use the story of the Good Samaritan to demonstrate the point. (See Luke 10:25-37.) Make a list of ways to be a better neighbor at church, in class, at home, during activities, and in the community.
- Action prayer: Have a "brownie circle" closing. Each person crosses arms and joins hands with the person on either side to form a complete circle. Leader or child can offer prayer for the group and for each to be good neighbors this week. On a signal, keeping handholds, take arms up over head, and turn to face the outside of circle. Pray to send off and release!

Week 6: My Whole Self

My whole self is God-made and God-loved and needs care, respect, and discipline.

- Verses: "'You shall love the Lord your God with all your heart, and with all your soul, and with all your mind, and with all your strength.' The second is this, 'You shall love your neighbor as *yourself.*' There is no other commandment greater than these" (Mark 12:30-31, author's emphasis).
- Theme: Taking good care of myself is a way to show God my love.
- Activity ideas: Use large pieces of poster paper and trace the outline of classmates lying in different poses. In small groups, label all the parts in the drawing. Prepare cards showing things we need to take care of ourselves (e.g., comb, soap, toothbrush, food, water, jungle gym, Bible, adults, car/bike/scooter, house, bed, etc.). Have each group sort the cards into two piles: care of outside vs. care of inside of self. (For youth, work as a group to order the five most important items to have on a deserted island.)
- Thinking things: What do we need to have or do to keep ourselves healthy? Are there things that are unhealthy to do? Does everyone have everything they need to be healthy? Is this true everywhere in the world?
- Action prayer: Form a "brownie circle" closing. Each student in turn tells one unique thing they are thankful for and then turns to outside of circle, one by one. The last student signals "break" or "go!"

Conclusion Week

- Verses: "'You shall love the Lord your God with all your heart, and with all your soul, and with all your mind, and with all your strength.' The second is this, 'You shall love your neighbor as yourself.' There is no other commandment greater than these" (Mark 12:30-31).

- Theme: Because God loves me, I can love God with my heart, soul, mind, strength and by the way I treat my neighbor and myself.
- Activity: Review the theme verse from memory. Create five stations or countries and call them Heart/Soul/Mind/Strength/Neighbor, respectively. Have students visit with their Loving God Passport. Have a different favorite activity from each week for students to do at the stations. Write a thank-you note to God (as a class or individually) in the passports. Ask someone to read his or her thank-you note or offer it as a closing prayer.
- Thinking things: How does each station remind me of God? How can it be a reminder all the time? How is my body a way I can take God with me? How is taking care of my body similar to saying thanks to God? For youth, discuss stewardship, self-respect, respect for others, and good decision-making.
- Action prayer: Form a circle. On inhale, move into the center as close as you can without touching; on exhale, move backward to form the larger circle. Repeat several times. Group members are beating (lub-dub), breathing (inhale-exhale), thinking (concentrate/rest), contracting/relaxing as a group, a symbol of the body of Christ. Place hands in the center and count, "1-2-3 Go God!"

About the Author

Wendy LeBolt, PhD, holds advanced degrees in cardiovascular physiology and exercise science but her profession, her mission and her ministry find their perfect intersection on the field of play. For nearly two decades she has been reaching out to young people and their families through her business, Fit2Finish. Wendy calls herself a Kinesthetic Christian, finding faith in the physical and the body-soul connection, inseparable. She and her husband Scot have three grown daughters and split their time between Williamsburg, Virginia, and Sarasota, Florida.